Fictions of the Past:
Hawthorne & Melville

Fictions Of The Past: Hawthorne & Melville

Alide Cagidemetrio

the Institute for

Advanced Study in the
Humanities

Distributed by
The University of Massachusetts Press

Copyright © 1992 Alide Cagidemetrio

Fictions of the Past: Hawthorne & Melville is a publication of the Institute for
Advanced Study in the Humanities at the University of Massachusetts
at Amherst

Distributed by
The University of Massachusetts Press
Box 429
Amherst, Mass. 01004
Printed in the United States of America
August 1992
LC 92-39609

ISBN 0-87023-861-2

Library of Congress Cataloging-in-Publication Data

Cagidemetrio, Alide.
    Fictions of the past: Hawthorne & Melville / Alide Cagidemetrio.
    197 pp. + xiv cm.
    Includes bibliographical references.
    ISBN 0–87023–861–2 (pbk.)
    1. Historical fiction, American—History and criticism.   2. Hawthorne,
Nathaniel, 1804–1864—Knowledge—History.   3. Melville, Herman,
1819–1891—Knowledge—History.   4. American Fiction—19th century—
History and criticism.   5. United States in literature.   I. Title.
PS374.H5C33   1993
813'.309—dc20   92–39609
                                                                         CIP

British Library Cataloguing in Publication data are available.

a mia madre, a mia figlia

Contents

Acknowledgements

I wish to thank the Institute for Advanced Studies in the Humanities and its Director, Jules Chametzky, for making the publication of this work possible. As a fellow of the Institute in 1990, I had the opportunity to benefit from the comments of a learned and sympathetic audience to the first draft of my Melville essay. Many are the mentors and friends, in Amherst and Cambridge, whom I wish to thank; and still many more are the mentors and friends in Italy, to whom goes my deepest gratitude. They will recognize in this work many a conversation, many shared ideas and projects or passionate reading encounters. To Sergio Perosa and Rosella Mamoli Zorzi I owe the privilege of having been their student, and to them is my greatest debt.

I am also grateful to Lauren Gwin who assisted in the editing process, Robert Levers who designed the cover, and Daniel Griffin who supervised the printing.

To thank one's family in print is a grateful task: my own has been supporting, understanding, patient, even when these were gifts hard to bestow. To my mother and my daughter this book is dedicated.

Preface

The specific study of forms does not in any way contradict the necessary principle of totality and history. On the contrary: the more a
system is specifically defined by its forms the more amenable it is to
historical criticism.

—Roland Barthes

This book is about a concern with the past. This concern originates
in the belief that discourses of the past are necessary to shape the
notion of the "new" that has dominated our modern age. The subject
of inquiry is here limited to two significant, and canonical, American
writers, Nathaniel Hawthorne and Herman Melville.

Both Hawthorne and Melville are writers of historical fictions, and
both contribute, in different degrees and in different ways, to a literary representation of the past that is foundational for our late twentieth-
century expectations about the relation between history and fiction.
Within the literary tradition established by Walter Scott's "Waverley
Novels", Melville's and Hawthorne's texts mark a significant departure: narrative "verisimilitude" is not, as in the classical historical
novel, dependent upon the representation of events of history, but it
rather depends upon referentiality to history. The notion of
"authenticity" is no longer founded on the evidence of historiographical accounts of the past but on a process of interpretation that renews
the signs of the past.

Hawthorne's *Legends of the Province-House*, and his unfinished
romances, and Melville's *Israel Potter* are read here as experiments in
writing the past "anew", in a cultural age that experienced an unprecedented acceleration towards the future and quickened the disappear-
ance of the signs of the past. Still it is the return of these signs that
appears to be an essential part of a vision of the future, for Hawthorne
and also for Melville.

Hawthorne's symbols of the past generate historical fiction, as in
The Scarlet Letter. After *The Scarlet Letter* Hawthorne abandoned a fiction set in the past for a fiction about the past. My focus is on the

forms of this transition: *The Legends of the Province-House* is seen as the early historical fiction that carries with it the method of a transformation. The last unfinished romances measure the extent of the transformation: writing about the past becomes writing about individual memory.

Hawthorne's own concern with the past was never separated from his concern with science and related modern technologies. My reading of Hawthorne confronts this apparent dichotomy and investigates the analogies between technological apparatuses (such as phantasmagoria or telegraph) and his expressive methods. These analogies speak for the "new" linked to the "old"; this connection supports the representation of a modern "historic consciousness" which, as Henry James pointed out, is the major legacy of Hawthorne's fictions of the past.

Melville's books of the past generate historical fictions, as in *Israel Potter*, and "Benito Cereno". *Israel Potter* is the first of Melville's fictions of the past; this novel rewrites an authentic historical source. As such it provides an excellent example of Melville's method of writing as reading. Different from the contemporary "Benito Cereno", the authentic book of the past is self-reflexively incorporated in Melville's 1854 novel: my focus is on Melville's narration as a process of reading (and interpreting) the past through a rewriting of the sources that define it. For Melville writing a historical novel has become writing about the interpretation of the past, the rhetoric of its discourses, and the signs that commemorate history in the present. In this Melville shows the other side of the "modern historic consciousness": the new is linked to the old, as for Hawthorne, but both are inventions with a purpose.

Writing the past anew in *Israel Potter*, Melville's purpose seems to be eminently political. Accordingly, my reading of *Israel Potter* investigates that novel's place within the tradition of American historiography, and within a contemporary urge towards the long waited for realization of prophetic destinies. *Israel Potter* is seen as a text that strives for the invention of a "usable past" that would turn historical failures into a delayed realization of the promise of history.

Both Hawthorne and Melville were two generations removed from the American Declaration of Independence. As the texts chosen here show, their concern with the past revolves around paradigmatic events, Migration and Revolution, which had become crucial in defining national identity. They both confronted, as their textual strategies prove, the possible contradictions between national value and historical failure. In doing so they both, in different ways, represented the past as a modern compromise: the past is an authentic presence because it potentially contains any future; on the other hand any future past comprehends both progress and regress, realized failure and unrealized expectation. Sometimes, as it happens with Hawthorne's unfinished romances, the pressure of renewed historical contradiction may shatter the vision; still Hawthorne's texts of the late fifties and early sixties and Melville's work of 1854 suggest parallel projects which deny the nationally acclaimed absence of the past in the land of the new and make, by contrast, the American past a past of universal value.

HAWTHORNE

Phantasmagoria.

Part One

The Phantasmagorias of Nathaniel Hawthorne

It is a world, this, of magic become *real*.

—Thomas Carlyle, *The French Revolution*

Confronted with Hawthorne's fictions, puzzled by the fact that they are not novels but romances, we have hesitated to place them in this world. For to do so, were we to assent to them, would be also to place ourselves in his world. Instinctively perhaps, we have resisted being drawn out of our world into his. Even ours, we say, is already too much with us. So we have allegorized, mythologized, psychoanalyzed, theologized — all to the end of deriving Hawthorne's symbols from a world which neither he nor we ever could have made.

—Roy Harvey Pearce, "Romance and the Study of History"

The sense of the past *is* your sense.

—Henry James, *The Sense of the Past*

ON PHANTASMAGORIAS AND HAWTHORNE

Ghostly visions characterize Hawthorne's fiction. There is a metaphor for these visions, phantasmagoria, which, though persistent in his work, has not received critical attention from Hawthorne's readers. Yet phantasmagoria is a crucial romantic term that refers both to the workings of imagination, and to its representation. Recent studies have connected phantasmagorias to the early nineteenth-century debate on seeing and ghost-seeing. This debate is seen as foundational both for modern psychology and for modern notions of visuality (Castle, 1988; Crary, 1990). "Phantasmagoria" and "modern" are indeed interchangeable terms in a classic of literary theory, Walter Benjamin's "Paris, Capital of the Nineteenth Century" (1935), and phantasmagorias were viewed as signs of the modern by visionary nineteenth-century writers. It is my intent to investigate such interpretative and historical connections between phantasmagoria and the modern, in order to account for Hawthorne's own ghostly visions, in the belief that these visions constitute the most striking feature of his contribution to the formation of a modern representation of reality.

Hawthorne was defined as "our contemporary" by Lionel Trilling (Trilling, 1964) and, indirectly, as a contemporary by Henry James, when he said, in his 1879 essay, that Hawthorne had "that faculty which is called now-a-days the historic consciousness" (James, 1967, 74). Taking its departure from both Trilling and James, my concern with Hawthorne's fictions of the past aims at exploring the ways in which Hawthorne formulated and represented a modern sense of history. In this perspective, phantasmagoria is a revealing metaphor which links together many of Hawthorne's own concerns: his concern with science and history, with the relation between imagination and representation, and with the blurring of the boundaries between illusion and reality. An investigation into the semantic history of phantasmagoria and into Hawthorne's own use of it may help to frame the analysis of his method of writing historical fiction and its transformation into a method of writing about the past as individual memory.

5

Phantasmagoria, as both Castle and Crary have convincingly argued, is a crossroad term for two modern ways of describing reality, one descended from optics, the other from psychology. Seeing *with* the eye, and seeing *through* the eye is after all not only an Emersonian transcendental concept, but also a materialistic, scientific notion. As the work of Henry James shows, the physical eye sees through the eye of psychology. Thus the supernatural becomes a function of a new mimesis, made verisimilar by the shared consumption of notions about reality.

At the very end of his career as a writer, in *Grimshawe*, Hawthorne gives an intriguing formulation to phantasmagoria. I take it to be Hawthorne's last declaration of poetics, embedded in a final representation of the familiar state between dream and reality. As the discussion of Hawthorne's unfinished romances is to show, Hawthorne here is meditating on his experimental representation of "psychic states" of consciousness; his use of phantasmagoria at this late stage, however, resonates with earlier uses in his work. The final use of phantasmagoria in Hawthorne's fiction provides the deconstructive point of view which informs my reconstruction of the metaphor's romantic and modern analogies, and of its place in the interpretation of Hawthorne's innovative method of representation.

<(Make this whole scene very dreamlike and feverish.)>
To say the truth, the traveller perhaps willfully kept hold of this strange illusiveness, and kept his thoughts from too harshly analyzing his situation, and solving the riddle in which he found himself involved. . . . He, meanwhile, would willingly accept the idea, that some spell had transported him out of an epoch . . . into a limbo where things were put away; shows of what had once been, now somehow parted, and still maintaining a sort of half-existence, a serious mockery; a state likely enough to exist just a little apart from the actual world, if we only know how to find our way into it. Scenes and events that have once stained themselves, in deep colours, on the curtain that Time hangs around us, to shut us in from eternity, cannot be quite effaced by the succeeding phantasmagoria, and sometimes, by a palimpsest, show more strongly than they (*Grimshawe*, 1977, 453).

Hawthorne alludes to earlier statements in "The Custom House" when he reformulates the "neutral ground", "a state likely enough to exist just a little apart from the actual world" as the space of fictional discourse (Swann, 1991, 178), while stressing its connection with the subjectivity of vision. Differently from the declaration of poetics in *The Scarlet Letter* the subjective view involved is not the narrator's but that of a character in dire straits whose perception of the process is one of "serious mockery". When the shift occurs from the character's point of view to the more generalized view of the narrator, a meditation upon time and memory follows as an indirect answer to the possibility of finding a way into that quasi-oneiric state where "the Actual and the Imaginary may meet". It is a meditation that casts memory as an anthropological category that interferes with, or surfaces in, credited if "illusive" shows of history.

The metaphorical field through which Hawthorne conveys meaning draws on stage ("curtain") and performance ("scenes"). This becomes especially obvious if we take "phantasmagoria" in its specific historical meaning. As the *Encyclopedia Britannica* (1911) puts it, "phantasmagoria" was, in fact, a name "invented by a certain Philipstal in 1802 for a show or exhibition of optical illusions produced by means of the 'projecting lantern' . . . The word has since been applied to any rapidly or strikingly changing scene or picture of the imagination". In Philipstal's exhibition the figures projected were rapidly made to appear smaller or larger than life, to be seen closer to, or farther away from the spectators, to dissolve or pass into each other.

"A constantly shifting phantasmagoria of figures" in Maule's Well either delights or terrifies Clifford, an "exhibition of phantasmagoric forms" are the sundry memories of her past life that relieve Hester "from the cruel weight and hardness of the reality" of her public exposure. And Pearl's "fancy" seems to follow the rules of a phantasmagoric show:

> It was wonderful, the vast variety of forms into which she threw her intellect, with no continuity, indeed, but darting up and dancing, always in a state of preternatural activity,—soon sinking down, as if exhausted by so rapid and feverish a tide of life—and succeeded by

other shapes of a similar wild energy. It was like nothing so much as
the phantasmagoric play of the northern lights (Hawthorne, 1983,
199).

Hawthorne's use of the term provides an instance of the current figurative meanings of the original phantasmagoric show. As Terry Castle
has noted "phantasmagoria" became almost instantly a figure for reverie, being readily perceived as a cogent analogy for mental or imaginative workings (Castle, 1988, 30; also Crary, 1990). In the light of
the new science the "so-called ghosts of the mind" could be turned
into real apparitions explained by the rationale of optical laws, the
same that were applied in the technical devices of the phantasmagorical show: concave mirrors, the arrangement of light, and fixed or
movable black curtains reproduced the workings of the human retina
and made the "illusions" collectively visible for large audiences.

"The phantasmagoria was invented . . . at a crucial epoch in the
history of Western ghost belief", when a shift in thought about the
nature of spectral apparitions occurred which reached its most glaring
formulation in the work of John Ferriar, *An Essay Towards a Theory of
Apparitions* (1813), as Castle points out. Hallucination (a word Ferriar
apparently popularized) was the result of the direct transition from the
image of memory to the "beholding of spectral objects", thus opening
the way for the poetics of reverie among romantic and symbolist writers which eventually would find its system in the Freudian theory of
dreams and its high expression in the Proustian work of memory
(Castle, 1988, 52-61).

The romantic obsession with states between wakefulness and sleep,
the stress on feverish or "nervous" states of perception, the fetishiza-
tion of chemicals such as opium and similia, seen as the instruments
able to enlarge the mind's properties, are linked to phantasmagoria as
the the representative vehicle of a "new" kind of reality. In *The Confessions of an Opium Eater* (1822), Thomas De Quincey suggests the link
between the phantasmagoric visions and social utopias; when assessing
the relation between the "phantasmagoria" of dreams and the
"dreaming" subject De Quincey extolls the superior dreaming faculty
of the philosopher, represented by such contemporary figures as Sam-

uel Taylor Coleridge and David Ricardo (De Quincey, 1851, 15-7). The claim to the centrality of the individual, which the *Confessions* explores by resorting to its experiential limits, is presented as different yet homologous to Ricardo's claim to economic individualism: "It seemed to me that some important truths had escaped even 'the inevitable eye' of Mr. Ricardo" (De Quincey, 1851, 107), writes De Quincey, setting his phantasmagoric eye in motion and prefacing its narration by the suggestion that what follows is the successful substitute for a previous attempt to write the "Prolegomena to all Future Systems of Political Economy".

Starting its opium visions at the druggist's in Oxford Street, and loitering through the streets of London, his "persona" is that of an earlier version of Walter Benjamin's *flâneur* who roams through Paris, taking in the features of the capital of the nineteenth century. Thomas Carlyle when describing his first impressions of London, in a letter to his wife on August 11, 1831, writes of the city and of his feeling of displacement in it in these terms:

> It is very sweet in the midst of this soul confusing phantasmagoria to know that I have a fixed possession elsewhere; . . . Expect no connected or even intelligible narrative of all the chaotic signs, sounds, movements, counter movements I have experienced since your lips parted from mine on our threshold—still less of all the higher chaotic feelings that have danced their wild torch dance within me (Froude, 1882, 165).

In Carlyle's eyes phantasmagoria is an analogy for both the urban scene and the response of his own inward world: the cityscape "disorder", the modern chaotic movements of the metropolis, are conveyed through the metaphor that thus becomes a substitute designation for London itself. In those same years another optically based form of entertainment, the panorama, underwent a similar metaphorical transformation; it was to convey the idea of an order projected over the urban scene by the reproduction of the principles of continuity of vision, while the phantasmagoria represented the principles of dissociation, discontinuity, and chaos.

9

In the wake of these chaotic romantic sensibilities and earlier *flâneurs*, Walter Benjamin's historically-oriented cultural mind casts phantasmagoria as the metaphor that expresses the sensation of "vertige caractéristique pour la conception que le siècle dernier se faisait de l'histoire", which is made visible ("sensible") in the century's "new forms":

> les formes de vie nouvelles et les nouvelles créations à base économique et technique que nous devons au siècle dernier entrent dans l'univers d'une fantasmagorie. Ces créations subissent cette "illumination" non pas seulement de manière théorique, par une transposition idéologique, mais bien dans l'immédiateté de la présence sensible. Elles se manifestent en tant que fantasmagories (Benjamin, 1982, 1, 60).

For Benjamin the phantasmagoric condensation of time and space induces the *flâneur*'s vertigo of a immediate, sensible appropriation of the past and the distant. It is the vertigo of the universalizing bourgeois strategy of dominion over reality in new forms that contain the opposites of a vision of progress, and the damning perception that nothing is new or original. Benjamin's Baudelaire, the type of the *flâneur*, "illuminates" the anguish of the individual as both protagonist and onlooker of phantasmagorias: the project of the modern hero as a "first person singular", defined by his specific, unique traits is haunted by the law of repetition of the same which, Benjamin suggests, is the law of repetition of the market forces made visible as phantasmagorias of time and space.

> Hawthorne a fait une découverte psychologique assez importante, c'est que la sensibilité est la fonction dominante de l'âme, celle qui commande toutes les autres fonctions et domine tous les organes moraux. L'état nerveux est l'état permenente de l'âme; *sa sensibilité défie toute comparaison . . . la fantasmagorie d'un mauvais rêve la torture comme un malheur réel* (Montague, 1860, 685; emphasis added).

This is from Émile Montague's essay on Hawthorne, which Henry James attacked as a superficial and unjust accusation of pessimism levelled against the American forefather. "Un romancier pessimiste en Amérique" appeared in August 1860 in the *Revue des deux mondes*. Besides showing agreement with the undisclosed authority of Edwin

Percy Whipple's views on Hawthorne's work—"gloomy" and endowed "with the morbid vitality of a despondent mood"—in the May 1860 issue of the *Atlantic Monthly*, Montague's piece bristles with similarly undisclosed references to Charles Baudelaire.

The *Revue des deux mondes* had first published Baudelaire's poems in 1855. The *Fleurs du Mal* were introduced with an elaborate cautionary note by its editors. While the merit of the work is cast within the enlarged horizons of modern times, its morality is defended from possible attacks on the ground of an all pervasive sense of "grief" (*Revue des deux mondes*, 10, 1855). The poems were nonetheless perceived as scandalous and in 1857 their book publication led to Baudelaire's conviction on issues of indecency. While Gustave Flaubert was acquitted of the same charge for *Madame Bovary*, Baudelaire was found guilty of producing "immoral" work. The *Revue des deux mondes* was a prime suspect in bringing about degeneracy. In such a climate, Montague's portrait of Hawthorne is understandably a passionate defense of his "pessimism" as a moral quality that emanates from "fleurs de cimitière", "fleurs bizarre", distilled from the "essence et l'aroma", le "parfum énervant" of his work. The reader can recognize in his phantoms "ses frères", as Hawthorne himself was implicitly recognized by Montague as Baudelaire's brother. It is a recognition confirmed in decadent France both by Théophile Gautier who stresses the power of Baudelaire's lines to evoke Hawthorne and his poisonous flowers in "Rapaccini's Daughter" and, later, by Walter Benjamin himself, who cites Gautier's comment on Hawthorne in his scrapbook for the Baudelaire essay (Benjamin, 1982, 1, 359).

In January 1860 *La Revue contemporaine* had published "Un mangeur d'opium", Baudelaire's abridged translation-commentary of De Quincey's work. Baudelaire interprets De Quincey's "creative power of the eye" as transforming "en réalités inévitables tous les objets de ces rêverie". Baudelaire then adds a phantasmagoria of his own to De Quincey's:

> Toute cette fantasmagorie, si belle et si poétique qu'elle fût en apparence, était accompagné d'une angoisse profonde et d'une noire mélancolie (Baudelaire, 1976, 183).

Montague's own comment on Hawthorne's phantasmagoric sensibility sounds like an echo of Baudelaire's echoing, in turn, De Quincey. In his 1964 monograph, Jean Normand urges a reading of Hawthorne in the light of Baudelaire; his view of Hawthorne's work—as the expression of a cinematic vision—is conveyed in terms connected to the archeology of optics. Hawthorne's represented consciousness is "like an eye that has become, in its turn, a projector, and is able to people the entire universe with its images in the manner of a magic lantern. Any image is at the same time both interior and projected, and the ground of all creation, as of all thought, is a double space, at once concave, reflected and reflecting (cave and mirror), and also convex, penetrated and measured by an imaginative flight" (Normand, 1970, 154).

Reading Hawthorne through Baudelaire—in itself a fascinating field of inquiry, with large reverberations on the often neglected cultural European-American exchanges at mid-century—can illuminate Hawthorne's own phantasmagoric analogy, as well as James's later curious simplification of Montague's essay. James's criticism of it appears more than superficial when his own "passionate observers" reveal a similarity to Baudelaire's "painters of modern life" (Bell, 1991, 33; 157).

Consistently Montague makes Hawthorne a discoverer of "la maladie de l'âme", itself the source of a new view of morality. Concerned as he always was with morality, James wrote the Hawthorne essay in 1878, when engaged in learning the French realists' lesson and debating fiction as a moral art (Perosa, 1984). James implicitly defends Hawthorne against possibly "immoral", even if undeclared, comparisons, not by engaging Montague on his own ground but by dismissing his essay as "superficial" criticism. Yet James's famous statement on Hawthorne's morality, defined as his quality of penetration into "man's soul and conscience", comes after the dismissal of Montague, and basically shares the French critic's stress on Hawthorne's "découverte psychologique":

The charm—the great charm—is that [the tales] are glimpses of a great field, of the whole deep mystery of man's soul and conscience. They are moral, and their interest is moral; they deal with something more than accidents and conventionalities, the surface occurrences of life. The fine thing in Hawthorne is that he cared for the deeper psychology, and that, in his way, he tried to become familiar with it. This natural, yet fanciful familiarity with it, this air on the author's part of being a confirmed *habitué* of a region of mysteries and subtleties, constitutes the originality of his tales . . . The author has all the ease, indeed, of a regular dweller in the moral, psychological realm; he goes to and fro in it as a man who knows his way. His tread is a light and modest one, but he keeps the key in his pocket (James, 1967, 72).

Naturally and yet fancifully familiar with the deeper psychological world, Hawthorne is, in James's view, a *"habitué"*, a "regular dweller" in the realm where psychology is turned into a new moral category capable of containing disorder.

In Benjamin's terms, James's "regular dweller" can be read as a sanitized and sanitizing version of the *flâneur-turned-habitué* whose discovery of the centrality of seeing as a psychological function is developed into the ability of forging an image of the "real", thus projecting a new form of dominion over it. Knowing his way, he can "inhabit" or own the world. Hawthorne's modesty, even his "provincialism", is the native quality that prevents or "naturally" overcomes excesses by a form that makes them "familiar". James's own *flâneurs* could be read in this light, as characters roaming the streets of European cities bent on familiarizing, through a parallel roaming of their perceptive consciousnesses, the effects of ravaging modern events such as the spatial contraction of different worlds (the "international theme"), the spreading of viruses like anarchism or feminism, the containment of social changes in marriage contracts, or of individualism as an asocial practice that may include the extremes of adultery, or even of murder. James's own "reticence" in his reading of Montague's essay, not less than in his own writings, can indeed be a matter of "taste", as Barbara Melchiori has shown (Melchiori, 1974, 3-29), and it may also be the paradoxical method that contains, without denying them, the "totality of impressions" that are surfacing in the "eye" of the middle class protagonist of his fictions.

It is the paradox of the modern field of vision that Benjamin sees in the phantasmagoric forms of contemporary "things". James's own characteristic "things" stand out in his 1904 assessment of Hawthorne's "value":

> . . . he saw the quaintness or the weirdness, the interest *behind* the interest, of things, as continuous with the very life we are leading, or that we were leading . . . round about him and under his eyes; saw it as something deeply within us, not as something infinitely discon-nected from us; saw it in short in the very application of the specta-tor's, the poet's mood, in the kind of reflection the things we know best and see oftenest may make in our minds (James, 1984, 471).

In 1904 James, engaged in the writing of *The Golden Bowl*, sounds more conscious of the relation between Hawthorne's method and his own, and of Hawthorne's stand as a classic. And in his own definition a "classic" writer is the one judged by posterity not in the light of the trivial developments of literature (the "journalistic" fashion that Haw-thorne, too, saw, in its earlier stages), but in that of the characteris-tic ones, of "the better machinery" that the later generation could perfect, pulling "stronger wires" out of their "reflections" than the earlier writer's "romantic" spirit did.

The "bright light of the latter end of the nineteenth century", James wrote in 1889, through the persona of the international *flâneur* Darcy—whose name is in itself a reference to the order eventually composed in Jane Austen's *Pride and Prejudice*—has brought about a "rough process" of adjustment:

> Our modern intimacy is a very new thing, it has brought us face to face, and in this way the question comes up for each party of whether it likes, whether it can live with the other. The question is practical, it's social now; before it was academic and official. Newspapers, tele-graphs, trains, fast steamers, all the electricities and publicities that are playing over us like a perpetual thunderstorm, have made us live in a common medium, which is far from being a non-conductor (James, 1984, 81).

Darcy's metaphor for the common "medium" is the "Grand Hotel of Nations", a metaphor whose real space is not different from Benjamin's "universal exhibition" halls. They are, Benjamin writes, the visible space where use value yields to exchange value, where individuals can abandon themselves to the intimacy of the shared consumption of entertainment, and thus become part of the compromise between utopia and cynicism that the exhibits celebrate. In its turn Benjamin's metaphor for such real space is the phantasmagoria whose literal meaning is that of the early century: a new, technological, multimedial form of entertainment.

As the pioneering work of M. H. Abrams has taught us, metaphors are never innocent. When discussing the ubiquitous presence of eye-related analogies in romantic poetics and texts, their striving towards the suggestion of a "single vision" that would comprehend both the inner and outward eye, Abrams writes:

> The shift is from physical optics to what Carlyle in the title of one of his essays called "Spiritual Optics", and what Blake and others called "Vision". Since the perception of a new world was the criterion of success in life—the condition of experience which writers who retained the traditional vocabulary called "redemption"—it will be useful to identify the principal ways in which this triumph of vision over optics was said to manifest itself . . . I discussed the major and inclusive way, the transformation of a discrete, dead, and alien milieu into a human, integral, and companionable milieu in which man finds himself thoroughly at home. But there are several supplementary ways in which the eye, altering, was said to yield, at least momentarily, a recreated world (Abrams, 1971, 377).

For the generations following the heroic romantic age it became increasingly difficult to find themselves "at home", in a "companionable milieu", as Abrams points out by selecting the obvious examples of Baudelaire's and of Rimbaud's poetics of the "disordering of the senses". However, the romantic "need for a revolution of seeing that made the object new", Abrams recognizes, survives in the twentieth century, if "sometimes distorted", in the categories of "freshness of sensation, revelatory moments, and the rectified outlook which inverts the status of the lowly, the trivial, and the mean" (Abrams, 1971, 411). The romantic strategies of seeing are inseparably linked to the new notions of "visuality" emerging by the unified scientific and philosophical debate on the properties of human sight, as Jonathan Crary has brilliantly shown (Crary, 1990). Phantasmagoria was the evidential proof both of the soundness of the new laws of optics and of the results of psychological investigation on ghost-seeing. By analogy it projected the very concept of the modern both on the workings of the imagination and on the world scene. By setting on stage the optical principles of the camera obscura the phantasmagoric shows concurred in the formation of the spectator's revolutionary vision of the "new things". It was a medium able to "conduct" to the subjective contemplative eye the longed for familiarity with the modern sense of the real, fixing in the immediacy of perception both the past and the present, the near and the distant, weirdness and rationality, utopia and social compromise, persistence and change.

If metaphors are never innocent, a reading of Hawthorne is justified which aims at showing that the shift operated by the optical metaphor does indeed, as Abrams noted, mark the "triumph of vision", but not over optics. The force of vehicles such as the phantasmagoria is to offer an evidential proof and a scientific rationale for shaping and enlarging the spatial and temporal domain of the "real".

PHANTASMAGORIC SHOWS AND THE POETICS OF ROMANCE

Hawthorne's was an age of phantasmagoric shows, the public performances of which survived, in different forms, for more than half a century. A successful form of entertainment, phantasmagorias and their technical apparatuses were constantly improved upon since their first appearance in Paris in 1798 (four years before the *Encyclopedia Britannica* dates them) to as late as 1862 and beyond, when J. H. Pepper created a sensation in London by improving upon the so called Dircksian phantasmagoria in a staged production of Charles Dickens's

"The Haunted Man". They have been used since as common stage machines for creating "eerily realistic" effects (Morley, 1952, 185-90).

Hawthorne himself might have had more than one opportunity of being part of the audience. He might have seen the "Phantasmagoria" at Crombie's Hotel in Salem (Ryan, 1958), or the shows put up in the "Phantasmagoria Room" of the Boston Museum (Clapp, 1853). As Benjamin Lease suggests, in *The Birthmark* (1843) Hawthorne describes Aylmer's staged phantasmagoria from the point of view of the spectator (the secluded Georgiana) with the flair of the *connaisseur* (Lease, 1976, 138):

> Airy figures, absolutely bodyless ideas, and forms of unsubstantial beauty, came and danced before her, imprinting their momentary footsteps on beams of light. Though she had some indistinct idea of the method of these optical phenomena, still the illusion was almost perfect . . . Then again, when she felt a wish to look forth from her seclusion, immediately, as if her thoughts were answered, the procession of external existence flitted across a screen. The scenery and the figures of actual life were perfectly represented . . . (Hawthorne, 1982, 771).

The effects of reality that Aylmer has produced are indeed powerful in Georgiana's eyes. As another connaisseur, Edgar Allan Poe, recognized these were effects much needed in the field of modern entertainment. In 1844 Poe complained about the sluggishness of American impresarios who did not use phantasmagoric effects in their productions, as the Germans had done in a production of *Macbeth* in which a "shadowy figure" was made to appear in Banquo's chair, by the optical means devised by Enslen. "Intense effect was produced", writes Poe, and he comments: "I do not doubt that an American audience might be electrified by the feat" (Poe, 1984, 1336). Such a theoretician and master of effects as Poe, whose tales—"Ligeia", for example, which bears strong resemblances to Hawthorne's "Birthmark"—dwell on phantasmagoric settings, was of course particularly sensitive to a medium producing a representation that substituted effects for the staged, "mimic" presence of living actors.

By making the theatrical space a "camera obscura", or a "magic box", phantasmagorias could project a "totality of effects" on onlookers. At the same time the performance was the result of a concurrence of different means, mirrors, slides of lanterna magica, live actors and sounds. All these would be invisible to the audience, while the actors in the pit would not see the effects produced by their bodies and movements reflected by the concealed mirrors and projected upon the stage. Their know-how about the workings of the optical instruments was the substitute for their lack of an actual vision of the stage.

It is the know-how for producing effects which is central to the self-reflexive descriptions of phantasmagorias by their "inventors", whose constant preoccupation is to claim their scientific and therefore objectively verifiable foundations. Étienne Gaspard Robertson, the Belgian inventor of both panoramas and phantasmagorias and, apparently, of the latter word itself, took pains to explain the hidden workings of phantasmagorias in his autobiography. Doctor Pepper introduced his haunted man with a learned lecture. The man whose phantasmagoric techniques J. H. Pepper supposedly plagiarized, Henry Dircks—a Liverpool scientist who had given the report of his improved mechanism at the 1858 British Association for the Advancement of Science meeting—published a book, *The Ghost! As Produced in the Spectre Drama*, subtitled "popularly illustrating the marvelous optical illusions obtained by the apparatus called the Dircksian Phantasmagoria" (1863). All these writers felt obliged to explain illusionary techniques, in order to upgrade their shows, by pointing to their scientific base and distinguishing themselves from impostors. By doing so, they also placed themselves and their rational explanations within a larger educational process which popularized new concepts of vision. As Jonathan Crary argues, the change in theories of visuality which took place in the early nineteenth century, as a result of the investigations on the human eye, shifted the field of vision from the Lockean "tabula rasa on which orderly representations could be arrayed" to a "surface of inscription on which a promiscuous range of effects could be produced" (Crary, 1991, 96). Such a range of effects could become acceptable precisely because a new culture of what was becoming "visible" was made available through instruments like the "magic box" and shows like the phantasmagoria.

Phantasmagorias, which date back to the French Revolution, are consistently defined as part of a process in which the findings of modern science are translated into modes of consumption, into "representations" inseparable from scientific or technological achievements. As ancestral forms for motion pictures they could be seen as marking the beginning of that desire, in Walter Benjamin's words, "of contemporary masses to bring things 'closer' spatially and humanly, which is just as ardent as their bent toward overcoming the uniqueness of every reality by accepting its reproduction" (Benjamin, 1969, 223). As a reviewer of Dircks's book noticed, the reader will be told "how the spectre was raised, and how we may ourselves at pleasure call spirits from the vasty deep", once provided with the proper instruments and the proper know-how.

Such access to means of production and their scientific principles allows for a change in the concept of verisimilitude: by owning the techniques of illusions, illusions themselves are made verisimilar, that is part of a shared knowledge about reality. Phantasmagorias can become evidence for what the "eye" is enabled to see. The reality of what is seen is guaranteed both by the avowal of the individual uniqueness of vision and by the generalized scientific principles which explain it, thus fulfilling both the requirements of being plausible and having the appearance of truth. Paradoxically, the produced reality of the show can claim verisimilitude even when it borders on the extreme of illusion because the show can, at the same time, assess its autonomy and its claim at being a possible, produced, image of the world.

This is true also for the literary work to which it is metaphorically linked. Crary recalls Theodor Adorno's usage of the term "phantasmagoria" in the description of the poetics of the 1850s as indicating:

> the occultation of production by means of the outward appearance of the product . . . this outer appearance can lay claim to the status of being. Its perfection is at the same time the perfection of the illusion that the work of art is a reality *sui generis* that constitutes itself in the

realm of the absolute without having to renounce its claim to image the world (Crary, 1991, 132).

Hawthorne's own working definition of romance in the preface to *The Blithedale Romance* lends credence to such considerations and expands them as to include Benjamin's own use of "phantasmagoria" as the *locus* of the surge and the defeat of the utopian element embodied by the Paris Commune (Benjamin, 1982, 1, 74):

> In short, his present concern with the Socialist Community is merely to establish a theatre, a little removed from the highway of ordinary travel, where the creatures of his brain may play their phantasmagorical antics, without exposing them to too close a comparison with the actual events of real lives . . . [A] Faery Land, so like the real world, that, in a suitable remoteness, one cannot well tell the difference, but with an atmosphere of strange enchantment beheld through which the inhabitants have a propriety of their own (Hawthorne, 1983, 633).

Phantasmagoria is invoked to express the "wider latitude" of romance: it lends plausibility to the artifact's claim to autonomy from reality, to its claim to become a "kind of rival creation as regards our life and our world" (Perosa, 1984, 59). At the same time the "visibility" of phantasmagoria enlarges the scope of what can be perceived (and contained) as "real". The notion of "likeness" between text and world discards a concept of plausibility based on similarity, substituting one of blurred differences, on the proposition that "one cannot well tell the difference" between scenic or fictional illusion and actual experiences. The degree of plausibility that is allowed to the romancer, Hawthorne's constant preoccupation, is no longer dependent on "a too close comparison" to actual life, but relies instead on the reader and writer sharing the effects of a common process of vision, within a "theatrical" space of representation.

By centering artistic endeavor on blurred differences, Hawthorne's notion of romance can be described within Todorov's definition of the fantastic as the hesitation between two categories, the "actual" and the "imaginary". Yet Hawthorne also undermines hesitation by evoking a beholder within shared concepts of vision that enable to see *through* strange enchantments a modified notion of the real.

20

In the unfinished romances Hawthorne's aim was, in his own words, to achieve "imaginative" or "romantic probability", "something monstrous yet within nature" (Davidson, 1964, 148-9). This was part of a modern strategy of representation of phenomena previously considered as magic and perceived as supernatural. Hawthorne's "Faery land" may be almost Spenserian. Yet his phantasmagoria is not only associated with the "charming poetic freedom of romance", as Terry Castle puts it (Castle, 1988, 47), but also with the rationalization of magic in such works as Sir David Brewster's *Letters on Natural Magic* (1832). Brewster's scientific description of "Spectral Illusions" points to Hawthorne's elaborate autobiographical representation of the narrator's dealings with his "illusive guests" in *The Scarlet Letter:*

> In darkness and in solitude, when external objects no longer interfere with the pictures of the mind, they become more vivid and distinct; and in the state between waking and sleeping, the intensity of the impression approaches to that of visible objects. With persons of studious habits, who are much occupied with the operations of their own minds, the mental pictures are much more distinct than in ordinary persons; and in the midst of abstract thought, external objects even cease to make any impression on the retina . . . In such cases, however, the philosopher is voluntarily pursuing a train of thought on which his mind is deeply interested; but even ordinary men, not much addicted to speculations of any kind, often perceive in their mind's eye the pictures of deceived or absent friends, or even ludicrous creations of fancy, which have no connection whatever with the train of their thoughts. Like spectral apparitions they are entirely voluntary, and though they may have sprung from a regular series of association, yet it is frequently impossible to discover a single link in the chain. If it be true then, that the pictures of the mind and spectral illusions are equally impressions on the retina, the latter will differ in no respect from the former, but in the degree of vividness by which they are seen (Brewster, 1843, 55-6).

Touching upon the light effects of the glaring sun in bringing about optical illusions, Brewster deals with illusions of colors and quotes a recorded instance of a family of nine people poisoned by black henbane to whom *"every object appeared . . . as red as scarlet".* I am not suggesting that Brewster's *Letters* provide the source for Hawthorne's scarlet letter, but they do provide a possible interpretative key for his description of the fictional process at whose center of invisibility the scarlet letter is situated. It was Brewster's contention that,

> "the mind's eye" is actually the body's eye and that the retina is the common tablet on which both classes of impressions are painted, and by means of which they receive their visual existence according to the same optical laws. Nor is this true merely in the case of spectral illusions: it holds good of all ideas recalled by the memory or created by the imagination (Brewster, 1843, 53-4).

Hawthorne's "neutral ground" could be seen as the space of the balance between the body's eye and the mind's impressions. In Brewster's view in "the healthy state of the mind and the body the relative intensity of these two classes of impressions on the retina are nicely adjusted" (54). Far from being the token of a deranged imagination such balance is taken to be the normal fare of human beings, *not different* from the "observations of external objects during the twinkling of the eyelids".

The *Letters on Natural Magic* continue with one of the most famous descriptions of the applications of these principles in the visible reproduction of the phantasmagoria. Phantasmagoria as an artifact is forcefully presented through a concept of "likeness" founded on experiential reality and scientific method. By means of light, and plane and concave mirrors, one can produce a likeness to what was perceivable in everyday life, by anybody. As a working likeness of the body's eye, explains Brewster, the new medium blurs the difference between real and illusionary worlds through the perception of its effects as "likely" in the eye of the beholder. Its "magic" ultimately fits the category of explained supernatural, but with differences in degree and substance: supernatural-turned-natural appearances are not excesses, but effects that can be mechanically reproduced.

Brewster, the author of the essay on animal magnetism in the 1821 *Encyclopedia Britannica*, was a well-known and widely quoted authoritative scientist and inventor. He was also a successful popularizer of scientific beliefs as the several editions of his *Letters* prove. Hawthorne himself borrowed a copy of them on September 19, 1837; and on October 7th he recorded in his notebook:

> Distant clumps of trees, now that the variegated foliage adorn them, have a phantasmagorian, an apparition-like appearance. They seem to be of some kindred to the crimson and gold cloud-islands. It would not be strange to see phantoms peeping forth from their recesses (Hawthorne, 1972, 156).

Besides being intertextually linked to Brewster's descriptions of cloud-islands in his letter on "airy illusions", this journal description of natural scenery records the perception of the optical effect—the phantasmagorian, apparition-like appearance—of autumn trees, rather than detailing their physical qualities. Once the principle of optical effect is accepted in the description of a real scene, even stranger effects, like appearing phantoms, would no longer seem strange. The shift in focus reorients the logic of descriptive contiguity: trees perceived as "real" phantasmagoric forms can be made contiguous with imagined ghosts. The subject, as onlooker, is stylized as the recipient of the effect as well as the willful agent in furthering its consequences since they appear not unlikely even to the body's eye.

At least two of Hawthorne's contemporaries described his work as that of a beholder of phantasmagorias he himself operates. In 1864, George William Curtis wrote that Hawthorne's "genius broods entranced over the evanescent phantasmagoria of the vague debatable land in which the realities of experience blend with ghostly doubts and wonders"; and in 1870 an anonymous critic saw him as "looking" upon his characters who are "essentially phantasmagorias" projected through a "magic lantern, so that the instrument shows you only their shadows" (Crowley, 1970, 441, 465). For such readers references to phantasmagoria still retained a literal dimension; phantasmagoria is the access word for the shared perception of the "real" existence of a "vague debatable land", or for the identification of the "neutral ground" with a ground common to all. Believing, along with his readers, that the difference between illusionary and real worlds could be blurred, Hawthorne did indeed envision a kind of proto-"magical" realism: the strength of Hawthorne's romance may well be, as Henry James felt, in a "neutral ground" that makes separate yet equally real worlds seem "continuous" to each other.

HISTORY AS PHANTASMAGORIA

In Walter Benjamin's view, the legacy of the nineteenth century lies in the production of visible forms that embody both the realization of a project of dominion over the world and the "fantasmagorie de l'histoire elle même". David Brewster's *Letters on Natural Magic* are addressed to Walter Scott, the great wizard of historical novels, as a tribute to Scott's insights in his *Letters on Demonology and Witchcraft* (1830). Brewster's dedication to Scott presents the *Letters* as a plea for dispelling superstitions in the name of reason, history and politics:

> The subject of Natural Magic is one of great extent, as well as of deep interest. In its widest range, it embraces the history of governments and the superstitions of ancient times,—of the means by which they maintained their influence over the human mind,—of the assistance they derived from the arts and the sciences, and from a knowledge of the powers and the phenomena of nature. When the tyrants of antiquity were unable or unwilling to found their sovereignty on the affections and interests of the people, they sought to entrench themselves in the strongholds of supernatural influence, and to rule with the delegated authority of heaven. The prince, the priest and the sage were leagued in a dark conspiracy to deceive and enslave their species; and man, who refused his submission to a being like himself, became the obedient slave of a spiritual despotism, and willingly bound himself in chains when they seem to have been forged by the gods (Brewster, 1843, 14).

"Natural magic" embodies the rationalist faith in the progressive nature of science and political institutions whose ideal new world order, Brewster believed, would become a reality once the whole of mankind recognized that everything can be explained by science and eventually reproduced by technology. Étienne Gaspard Robertson had introduced in the same way the descriptions of his shows in Paris, in order to claim the enlightened use of the experience of optical illusion as a means to achieve a better understanding of history (the *"explica-*

tion de plusieurs faits historiques"). Philosophical musings are less apt to achieve such a goal than optical illusions as Robertson's rhetorical question makes apparent: "les ouvrages de dix Rousseau valent'ils un fait développé par l'experience?" (Robertson, 1831, 1, 205).

Representations of phantasmagorias worked as new means to "historicize" the French Revolution itself. The ghosts projected on the stage were often *revenants* whose revolutionary fate had doomed them to an untimely death. Nor was this a French phenomenon only: as William Clapp informs us in his *Record of the Boston Stage*, "Seignor [sic] Falconi", an Italian who plagiarized Robertson's invention, performed at the Federal Theatre a phantasmagoria described as "Ghost of the celebrated Charlotte Corde [sic], as when in the last act of stabbing Marat. She will appear a luminous body, enveloped in darkness, as large as life, and every feature distinguishable for the space of three or four minutes" (Clapp, 1853, 37).

The illusory experience had such a power over audiences that it was immediately singled out as a counterrevolutionary practice. Robertson quotes extensively from a satirical article, which appeared in *L'ami de Lois*, March 28, 1798, describing his first phantasmagoria. He does not deny the accuracy of the description of the show which evoked the Revolution under the guise of the "procès verbal" of May 31, through the magic words:

> *Conspirateurs, humanité terroriste, justice, jacobin, salut publique, exgéré, alarmiste, accapareur, girondin, moderé orleaniste* . . . À l'instant on voit s'élever des groupes d'ombres couvertes des voiles ensanglantés . . . La séance allait finir lorsqu'un chuan amnistié et employé dans les charrois de la république, demande à Robertson s'il pouvait faire revenir Louis XVI (Robertson, 1, 1831, 219-20).

His phantasmagoria was immediately closed down by the secret police. In his next show, this time in the provinces, Robertson made sure to show Robespierre's ghost annihilated by a portentous thunder when trying to leave his tomb, while the role of the enlightened and enlightening star is given to Napoleon, "le pacificateur", turned into a mythological figure by Athena, who crowns him.

From the spectators' descriptions of his phantasmagorias quoted by Robertson in his *Mémoires*, it is apparent that the realistic effect was stunning to the audience. They could not deny the evidence of their eyes; they did see the apparitions, saw them move as in real life. Goethe's widely echoed belief that the whole world was an optical illusion proved "true" for whole audiences but only to enhance its "haunting" larger-than-life quality: the figures would accentuate their illusionary effect by growing larger and then smaller than life, by "haunting" the viewers, too closely approaching them and immediately afterwards receding in space and disappearing, or transmigrating into the "corporeal" reality of each other. As a Bordeaux newspaper reported:

> Ce n'est plus un fantôme sans mouvement, sans vie, ce n'est plus un être imaginaire; c'est la nature elle-même animée et mouvante, mais sous des couleurs si inconnues à l'oeil, que le physicien, l'artiste, doutent encore si ce objet tient plus à l'art qu'à la nature (Robertson, 1831, 1, 280).

By exploiting and concealing both mirrors and lamps, the reality of illusion fostered a perception of art as reality which was, one would expect, heightened when the ghostly appearance of the unseen actors was linked to memory.

We know for example from Scott's *Letters on Demonology and Witchcraft*, that John Ferriar's explanations for apparitions were already current. The unconscious recollection of memories, of everyday-life incidents, encounters, details, writes Scott, may surface in the unaware subject's mind. The recognized property of the eye to see mental images may dispel any sense of fear in these, no longer strange, occurrences. In a narration strongly reminiscent of the rational tales of both Scott and Brewster, Hawthorne himself recorded his past experience with apparitions. The ghost of a certain Doctor Harris answered the request of Mrs. Ainsworth that Hawthorne should contribute his own "ghost tale" in exchange for her account of the bloody footstep on the threshold of Smithills Hall—the legend from which the English romances originated. In "The Ghost of Doctor

Harris" (1857), the apparition is explained as issuing from the memory of the old man and his habits; and the narrator's attitude verges on total impassivity, not even a shadow of fear clouding the objectivity of the report of this most strange happening.

It is not unlikely that the audience who saw Robertson's first phantasmagoria in 1798 could individually or collectively recall events and historical characters only imperfectly "forgotten" in the swift changes of those tremendous years. Marat, Charlotte Corday, Robespierre, the King, their murders or executions—Robespierre's had occurred only in 1794—were only a step removed from the changed scenes of the new Regime. If one looked at the phantasmagoric show and its reception only through a "gothic" perspective, its quality of bringing back memories and inducing the recognition of their "historicity" would be lost. It was indeed such "historicity", or the function of forging a collective memory of the Revolution, that the Napoleonic secret service clearly perceived when it not only stopped the show but also confiscated the technical appliances. Collective memory, one could surmise, found its representation in the eerie immediacy of characters and events belonging to a not too long ago "everyday" life in the spectators' minds. Represented through the phantasmagoric forms, memories could be both distanced as illusionary representations and, perhaps most importantly, seen as historical "excesses" which were nonetheless normalized by the modern reality of the medium.

As Abrams noticed, the "politics of vision" of Romantic writers is inseparable from visions of the Revolution. In the article "Sur la fantasmagorie", also quoted by Robertson in his *Mémoires*, the liberal journalist, playwright, and former revolutionary Louis Sebastien Mercier wrote:

> Le philosophe ne rejette point ce spectacle, qui, par le jeu et le combat de l'ombre et de la lumière, nous place entre les corps et les esprits, et, pour ainsi dire, sur les limites d'une autre monde; il ne le rejette point, surtout dans un temps où le moraliste sent plus que jamais le besoin d'entretenir le peuple d'une autre vie.
>
> Tout devient l'organe de la vérité, lorsque les vérités les plus utiles sont oubliées ou méconnues (Robertson, 1831, 1, 304-5).

27

In his *Nouveau Paris*, Mercier writes the story of the French Revolution as an eyewitness chronicle textured both by accuracy of details and grotesque representations whose deep structural principles he attributes to the Goethian motto "Tout est optique, ou jeu d'optique" (Mercier, 1800, 6, 138). The reality of the Revolution in its "extrême et continuelle mobilité optique" defies the historian's traditional role of an observer looking from a fixed point of view on a stable object (Mercier, 1800, 6, 144); the phantasmagoric analogy fosters a higher or truer-to-life representation of history than those inspired only by objective principles, now made obsolete by history as a subject of chaos and disorder, and by the concomitant need for establishing the centrality of the subjective view in the narration of things and men past.

Thomas Carlyle took up Mercier's challenge in his "poetic" representation of history in *The French Revolution* (1837). For him phantasmagoria becomes an analogy that both describes a state of things and structurally informs the telling of history as chaos. Carlyle's interest in phantasmagoria as a literary mode was awakened by Goethe's versions of it in "To Helena"—subtitled a "classic-romantic Phantasmagoria"—and later developed into a "revolutionary" type of poetics for historical writing as the principle of Disorder contained within the Order of the allegorical mode (Cumming, 1988).

In 1837 John Stuart Mill, who was instrumental in providing Carlyle with French sources for his work, hailed *The French Revolution* as a historical narrative superior to any preceding it. Though disparaging Hume's history by comparing it to a phantasmagoric show whose characters resemble "one another in being shadows", Mill sees the strength of Carlyle's work precisely in the "quaintness" of its method of presentation. Carlyle's history is not, like Hume's, a narration of factual records, but a representation of the "real world". As such *The French Revolution* affects the readers' "sentiments"; it does not impose a fixed opinion or interpretation, but forcefully binds the readers to form their own (Schneewind, 1965, 183-206).

As an opening to one of the most stylistically striking passages of his history, Carlyle does indeed prefigure his reader's response: "The

Reader, who looks earnestly through this dim Phantasmagory of the Pit, will discern few fixed certain objects; and yet still a few". He quotes Mercier, one of his constant sources, as the proponent of Goethe's maxim, "everything is optical", applied to history and sets his reader in the position of Mercier's historian. What follows is a literal phantasmagoria:

> He will observe in this Abbaye prison, the sudden massacre of the Priests being once over, a strange Court of Justice, or call it Court of Revenge and Wild Justice, swiftly fashion itself . . . So sit these sudden Courts of Wild Justice, with the Prison Registers before them; unwonted wild tumult howling all round; the Prisoners in dread expectancy within. Swift: a name is called; bolts jingle, a Prisoner is there. A few questions are put; swiftly this sudden jury decides; Royalist Plotter or not? In that case let the prisoner be enlarged with *Vive la Nation*. Probably yea; then still, let the Prisoner be enlarged, but without *Vive la Nation*; or else it may run, let the prisoner be conducted to La Force . . . Volunteer bailiffs seize the doomed man; he is at the outer gate; "enlarged" or "conducted" . . . into a howling sea; forth, under an arch of wild sabres, axes and pikes; and sinks, hewn asunder. And another sinks, and another; and there forms itself a piled heap of corpses, and the kennels begin to run red . . .
>
> A sombre-faced shifting multitude looks on; in dull approval, or dull disapproval, in dull recognition that it is Necessity (Carlyle, 1989, 3, 27-8).

Swift, sudden appearances and disappearances, the wry puns on the meanings of "enlarge", strengthen the immediacy of the representation, make it a haunting happening. The consistent use of the present tense gives *The French Revolution* a dramatic quality which unites in the immediacy of perception both narrator and reader. They are both turned into fictional spectators of crowded, distorted, optically fleeting scenes, in a "vision (spectral yet real)", as Carlyle puts it. The sounds themselves recall the eerie phantasmagorical effects of jingles and shrieks, while the silence of the crowd posits a further identification procedure for Carlyle's reader. He who looks earnestly through this "dim phantasmagory of the Pit" is silent, suggesting an analogy to the reception of actual phantasmagorias, the ritual silence of the theatrical space, but also stylizing reader and narrator as part of the the multitude of on-lookers of the revolutionary traumas. Mobile phantasmagorias capture scenes of history as "thousand-tinted Flame-image[s], at once veil and revelation". By giving the past their form the veil can be lifted in the immediacy of perception. Shocking effects act as counteragents to the "dulling" properties of time and may reveal that "there is nothing dead in this Universe" and that "change" does not excise the past from the present.

Carlyle's irony is directed against contemporary "sleepers": "Your Epimenides, your somnolent Peter Kraus, since named Rip Van Winkle" awaken to change but their dulled faculties prevent them from seeing continuities. The reader of his phantasmagorias instead sees anew the past in the present. Scenes and protagonists of past revolutions, be they "conspicuous or soon hidden", can be "seen" in the present. Or as Hawthorne would put it:

> Scenes and events that have once stained themselves, in deep colours, on the curtain that Time hangs around us, to shut us in from eternity, cannot be quite effaced by the succeeding phantasmagoria, and some-times, by a palimpsest, show more strongly than they (*Grimshawe*, 453).

Phantasmagoria as the representation of history can indeed transform reality into a phantasmagoric show that still hauntingly retains in the present stained scenes and events from the past, projected on a "curtain" that is significantly hung by Time "to shut us in from eternity" and therefore shuts us in historical time.

For Carlyle, Time is not constrained into spatial limits: its meta-phors (enveloped, deep-sunk, fashioned and woven) make it both a surrounding presence and a everlasting primal Force that constitutes the historical man who is "in the centre of two Eternities" (2;40). Carlyle's phantasmagorias enact History as the presence of the past within the still beneficial allegory of organic Time. A century later Benjamin reads in Auguste Blanqui's *Eternité par les Astres. Paris 1872* the allegory of organic time turned into the bleak hallucination of the "retour éternelle des choses". The phantasmagoria of modernity reveals the apocalyptic vision of revolutionary failure. Hawthorne's own formulation of "phantasmagoria" in *Grimshawe* can be read as post-Carlyle since a representation of the world as "fleeting" forms that contain the past is taken for granted. The acquired notion of the immediacy of past and present is not oriented towards an "eternal return" within transcendental Time, but within historical time. The question of the haunting return of "scenes and events" cannot be effaced by the representation of the phantasmagoria. There seem to be constants in the historical past that claim attention, lingering—as words in a palimpsest—within the scene of the phantasmagoria and as its residuum. The haunting persistence of such constants dramatically shakes the Order of allegory and renews the quest for a representation of history that might contain the tension between regression and progress, erasure and persistence and prevent the failure of revolutionary hopes by exorcizing haunted and haunting images.

PALIMPSESTS OF PHANTASMAGORIAS, OR THE MAKING OF HISTORICAL SYMBOLS: *THE LEGENDS OF THE PROVINCE-HOUSE*

Carlyle noted that words, as human events, do not disappear once written. Hawthorne's metaphorical relation between phantasmagoria and palimpsest equates words with the stained scenes of the past. Words written in the past survive in the present, as images of the past do in the phantasmagoric present.

Palimpsest is another recurrent romantic metaphor. In *Suspiria de Profundis* (1845) Thomas De Quincey details the passage to the modern figurality of this classic sign: "A palimpsest", he writes, "is a membrane or roll cleansed of its manuscript by reiterated successions" (De Quincey, 1851, 226). The property of *"receiving"* the impressions is coupled with the resistance of the material originally used—not paper but vellum. The costliness of the vellum made it so precious that a *"separate"* effort of inscription was required each time. This effort apparently erases previous writings, since the surface is written over. In the evidence of the processual quality of the vellum, the palimpsest shows its supremacy over printed books. Books printed on cheap paper lose the precious evidence of the process of both erasure and persistence repeated each time when the need for a new inscription arises. The palimpsest's figurative privilege is to convey the notion that to write anew is to write over previous texts. Its "endless strata", though covered in forgetfulness, can be revived by a visionary subject. Such has been in time the function of literature, an art that is, by romantic definition, visionary. As De Quincey writes:

> In the illustration imagined by myself, from the case of some individual palimpsest, the Grecian tragedy had seemed to be displaced, but was *not* displaced, by the monkish legend; and the monkish legend had seemed to be displaced, but was *not* displaced by the knightly romance . . . the traces of each successive hand writing, regularly effaced . . . have in the inverse order, been regularly called back: the footsteps of the game pursued, wolf or stag, in each several chase, have been unlinked, and hunted back through all their doubles (De Quincey, 1851, 237; 231).

Palimpsestes is the figurative title for Gérard Genette's archaeology of literary discourses. This title suggests Genette's method of investigating permanence of literary figures within subjective variations. Any literary work is in itself a "parody", or a "serious mockery" of other works. Theoretically, any text is characterized by its idiosyncratic intertextual and intratextual relations; historically, the conscious practice of intertextuality originates within the romantic awareness of the palimpsestic nature of tradition. While Herman Melville's work is the most glaring example of conscious intertextuality, Hawthorne's fictional fabric discreetly engages his reader in intertextual allusions. It is not my purpose to focus on the intertextual components of Hawthorne's fiction, but to link the notion of palimpsest to his "symbolic method" of representation of the past.

In Roy Harvey Pearce's view, Hawthorne's historicity is to be found "in an act deriving from the need to invent the symbol". This act is fictionally rendered in a process of symbol-making in which the reader must participate (Pearce, 1964, 232). As Pearce points out, Hawthorne's method strictly connects symbolic with historical representation in a common cultural act of interpretation of the past. To a post-structuralist, post-Hayden White reader a historical discourse based on "symbols" is even too familiar. Yet Hawthorne's rhetoric of history may still be perceived as an impure and ultimately incorrect way of writing historical fiction. In this view, within the literary tradition established by Scott, Hawthorne's work once again marks the tyrannical victory of metaphysical obsessions over historical concern. However, the persistence of a concern with history in his writings proves to be, as Pearce was the first to indicate, crucial in his symbolic method, thus calling for an assessment of Hawthorne's contribution to the tradition of historical fiction rather than for a dismissal of his work as a deviation from it.

Discussions of Hawthorne's symbolism have been crucial in shaping the debate on the historical or metahistorical quality of his writing. Recently reconstructive and deconstructive critical approaches have revived the issue in equally appealing readings. Michael Colacurcio's impressive study of Hawthorne's early tales (Colacurcio, 1984) makes a convincing argument for Hawthorne's obsessive, moral concern with history through the evidence of the countless historiographical allusions of his symbols, while Hillis Miller stresses "the possibility of the impossibility of unveiling" symbols in Hawthorne's work. In Hillis Miller's reading "The Minister's Black Veil" becomes the exemplum of textual indeterminacy and the vehicle of a notion of symbolism as the expression of the impossibility of "truly achieving Meaning" (Hillis Miller, 1991).

The unrecognized romantic foundation of Hillis Miller's notion of symbolism points, if anything, to an urgent need for a cultural history of symbolic concepts in modern times; it also revives a duality between literature and history—the one the domain of metaphysical parables, the other of historiography as a discourse of facts. This duality undermines Hillis Miller's own analytical intentions when he writes: "Only a rhetorical analysis of the relation between literature and history, an analysis recognizing the relation to be tropological, not merely conventional, grammatical, or logical, will escape some more or less subtle reaffirmation of historical determinism" (Hillis

Miller, 1991, 127). The fear of a New Historicist priority of history over literature denies to literary discourses the privilege of "writing" history or even "making" it, differently, yet not less effectively, or even more so, than historical discourses.

Consistent with De Quincey's elaborate claim to a collective textual memory activated by strained individual perceptions, Hawthorne's own symbolic method of writing history presupposes the attitude of the archaeologist, who uncovers the palimpsestic writings of literature *and* historiography, when selecting the symbols that can be re-written. In the writings of tradition, each equally true yet possibly unrelated, characteristic signs are made to appear—a scarlet letter, or a black veil and ancestral footsteps—which, as Hawthorne himself suggests and exegesis has debated, are referred to some source, be it legendary, or historiographical. Turned into symbols, such signs elude, however, the final proof of their origin, and thus become themselves the signs of an ongoing cultural process of making historical meaning in a literary narration.

> A license must be assumed in brightening the materials which time has rusted, and in tracing out the half-obliterated inscriptions on the columns of antiquity; fancy must throw her reviving light on the faded incidents that indicate character, whence a ray will be reflected, more or less vividly, on the person to be described (Hawthorne, 1982, 12).

Thus in "Sir William Phips" (1830) Hawthorne introduced his palimpsest figure. The light reflections may have the property of De Quincey's vellums. They may show the "inscriptions". Incidents that indicate "character", and prove to be more "true" to history than the accounts of the "historian" or the "biographer". Reformulating the notion of the poetic license of the historical romancer, Hawthorne both inscribes in his text a reference to the still dominant Scott-inspired poetics of historical fictions and signals a departure from them.

In both the "Preface" (1826) and the "Introduction" (1831) to *The Last of the Mohicans*, James Fenimore Cooper interpreted the fictional license as dependent on authenticated and well informed records of history. Historical truth, claimed by both historiography and fictional histories, is founded on the verisimilitude of the imaginative characters and incidents within the undisputable evidence of historical writing. Fiction's superiority ultimately resides in a successful compromise between invention and historiographical evidence, a compromise which does not dispute either such evidence or its method. In Hawthorne both historiographical evidence and method of history are a subject of investigation, as Michael Colacurcio has convincingly argued. Significantly "sources" are not the intertextual sign of historiographic evidence, as in Cooper or Scott. They are "buried", "half-obliterated", yet not "quite effaced". "Details of his country's past" are elected to the status of symbols, as John Becker has argued. Becker retains the opposition between "theory of history" and "allegorical" mode of presentation (Becker, 1971, 155). Still, as Carlyle's *French Revolution* shows, a discourse of history is not "contaminated" by allegory, but a new allegorical mode strives to give order to it, within an implicit theory of reality as phantasmagoria.

The inscriptions of Carlyle's writing in *The French Revolution* contribute to turn "details of his country's past" into symbols in *The Legends of the Province-House*. An early and intriguing instance of Hawthorne's symbol-making in historical contexts, the *Legends* were written and published a short time after the publication of the *French Revolution*. They appeared between 1838 and 1839 in the *Democratic Review*: the occasion was John O'Sullivan's invitation to offer a corroboration of the revisionistic anti-British, pro-democratic and future-oriented spirit of the new review with narrations of the national past. The *Legends* can be seen as a text containing the transition from a Scott-inspired model to a symbolic way of writing history; as has been remarked they open the way for the "typical illusion" of Hawthorne's major novel, *The Scarlet Letter* (Dauber, 1977, 87). The four tales are "framed" within the genre of historical fictions: a narrator is the recipient of old men's tales in the contemporary setting of the Boston Province-House, now a tavern. Yet the sequence of the tales is not determined by historical time, but by the apparent randomness of the surfacing of memories in the old men's minds. The narration is overtly symbolic: the symbolic nature of this or that word is often pointed out by their narrator as the sign of his interpretative writing over the oral accounts of his interlocutors.

The American Revolution is the historical event which, though not represented, informs the narration (Colacurcio, 1984; McWilliams, 1984; and Newberry, 1989). A revolutionary chronology frames the four legends in time (the first tale is set in 1775 and the last in 1780) and in each tale the Revolution is a constant referent that "historicizes" their collective theme—the "passing away" of the Colonial power.

In "Lady Eleanore's Mantle" such theme is most dramatically represented with a displacement in time and subject by focusing on the Great Plague of 1721. The Great Plague is in itself the symbol through which Hawthorne refers to the actual raging of the American Revolution, as both Colacurcio and Newberry have argued. A full quotation of the long plague narration of "Lady Eleanore's Mantle" is in order here, as an instance of Hawthorne's writing about the American revolution through the "palimpsest" of the phantasmagoric representation of the French:

> This was the appearance of a dreadful epidemic, which, in that age, and long before and afterwards, was wont to slay its hundreds and thousands, on both sides of the Atlantic. On the occasion of which we speak, it was distinguished by a peculiar virulence, insomuch that it has left traces—its pitmarks, to use an appropriate figure—on the history of the country, the affairs of which were thrown into confusion by its ravages. At first, unlike its ordinary course, the disease seemed to confine itself to the higher circles of society, selecting its victims among the proud, the well born and the wealthy, entering unabashed into stately chambers, and lying down with the slumberers in silken beds . . . But the disease, pursuing its onward progress, soon ceased to be exclusively a prerogative of the aristocracy. Its red brand was no longer conferred like a noble's star, or an order of knighthood. It threaded its way through the narrow and crooked street, and entered the low, mean, darksome dwellings, and laid its hand of death upon the artisans and the laboring classes of the town. It compelled rich and poor to feel themselves brethren, then; and stalking to and fro across the Three Hills, with a fierceness which made it almost a new pesti-

lence, there was that mighty conqueror—that scourge and horror of our forefathers—the Small-Pox . . . Graves were hastily dug, and the pestilential relics as hastily covered, because the dead were enemies of the living, and strove to draw them headlong, as it were, into their own dismal pit. The public councils were suspended, as if mortal wisdom might relinquish its devices, now that an unearthly usurper had found his way into the ruler's mansion. Had an enemy's fleet been hovering on the coast, or his armies trampling on our soil, the people would probably have committed their defense to that same direful conqueror, who had wrought their own calamity, and would permit no interference with his sway. This conqueror had a symbol of his triumphs. It was a blood-red flag, that fluttered in the tainted air, over the door of every dwelling into which the Small Pox had entered.

Such a banner was long since waving over the portal of the Province-House; for thence, as was proved by tracking its footsteps back had all this dreadful mischief issued (Hawthorne, 1982, 661).

The outbreak of the American Revolution in *Septimius Norton* echoes, almost thirty years later, the outbreak of the Plague in "Lady Eleanore's Mantle": " . . . this country was on the eve of a great convulsion which shook the country, and was hence communicated over the world, whence its profound vibrations have not yet ceased to be felt" (Hawthorne, 1977, 209). As Frederick Newberry has suggested, the Pox as the great leveler may have struck "a less jingoistic audience" as "a forecast of a leveling plague of more recent date, the Reign of Terror" (Newberry, 1989, 93). The "fierceness that made it almost a new pestilence" levels classes, public government is suspended, and the defense from a possible enemy invasion from the sea or from the land would have to be committed to the plague itself. This seems hardly a reference to the historiographical discourse of the American Revolution. A forecast of the French Revolution can be seen in Hawthorne's plague within a chronologically oriented interpretation, which, however, is at odds with a symbolic logic that condensates historical time and events in order to represent the "effects" of history and not history as the narration of factual sequences.

The common analogy of plague and revolution is explicitly defined as symbolic: its sign, the blood-red flag, links the 1721 plague to the

1789 French Revolution. The ominous "drapeau rouge" appears and disappears, as an anticipation of the Reign of Terror, in the second volume of Carlyle's *French Revolution*: in the eyes of the newly awakened Epimenedes, or "Peter Klaus, since named Rip van Winkle", it is the token of the passing away of the old power and the ensuing lack of government which turns the French into Bedlamites (Carlyle, 1989, 2, 289). The "drapeau rouge" is for Carlyle the "Flag of History" itself, the symbol that alludes not only to Terror but to the symbolic way of writing history in the aftermath of the Revolutionary era.

As the symbol of the very "Spirit of France", the flag "waxes ever more acrid fever-sick: towards the final outbursts of dissolution and delirium" (2, 128); yet it also speaks of Republicanism, whether standing for the painful process of drawing up the new Constitution or for the Martial law: "Howls of angry derision rise in treble and bass from a hundred thousand throats, at the sight of the Martial Law; which nevertheless, waving its Red sanguinary Flag, advances there . . . advances drumming and waving, towards the Altar of Fatherland . . . " (2, 183). And the finally drafted Constitution of the People is seen emerging as the "miraculous Standard of the Revolt of Men, as a Thing high and lifted up; whereon whosoever looked might hope healing" (2, 190). It is a hope shattered by turning such "Standard of the Revolt of Men" into an instrument "shamming death, *'faisant la mort'* ", of the Nation (2, 212), a "Social Clothing" that "shackles" France, menaced by the war with the rest of Europe. Yet the defense of the "Patrie en danger" is committed to its spirit (2, 223).

Similarly in Hawthorne's tale the defense of the people of Boston, from an enemy that is historically implausible in 1721, is committed to the plague. Its sign, the red flag, is deeply linked with the "social clothing" of Lady Eleanore. Her mantle is the apparent symbol of aristocratic Pride. Still, the sign of plague-and-revolution projects its historical reference on the imaginative sign, and it does so by extending their intertextual connectedness. In *The French Revolution* the flag is seen waving over the "Universal Insurrection of the Armed Population of Paris" which leads to the seizure of their Majesties, the country and its spoils. The author of *Sartor Resartus* does not fail to use symbolic garments in his historical narrative. "New clothes are needed" by the Queen planning the flight to Varennes. The "mantua-maker" is busy. The result is that a "hooded Dame", followed by others "hooded or shrouded", exits from the Royal Palace (2, 149; 152). Hiding in the garments will prove useless when the mob seizes their persons by discovering them, and leads them back as doomed captives in a grotesque procession.

Unaccountably Jervase Helwyse, the young American poet who is both a revolutionary spirit and the passionate lover of Lady Eleanore, offers to the mantled lady and to the aristocratic circle of friends of the Governor's, a sacrilegious drink in a "sacramental vessel" apparently stolen from Boston's Old South Church. He claims that by partaking of it Eleanore will prove that she has not withdrawn from "the chain of human sympathy". In Jervase's eyes the mantle is a mystic symbol; to the onlookers it becomes the historical symbol of the Plague, a replica of the red flag, only when he spills over it the stolen sacramental wine.

The mantle of Hawthorne's title is at first mentioned in relation to charm, beauty, and death. Only when Lady Eleanore wears it at the Colonial party in her honor, is its death-relation strenghtened: "and, perchance, it owed the fantastic grace of its conception to the delirium of approaching death". It is literally its maker's approaching death, but it also resonates with Carlyle's tainted feverish France moving "toward its final dissolution and delirium". The fateful contamination of the mantle eventually comes through the supposed agency of a maddened, sacrilegious Jervase Helwyse.

The revolutionary appropriation of "things sacred" is emphasized by Carlyle with a quotation from Mercier who describes the sacrilegious procession that, dancing at the festive sound of the Carmagnole, brought the church's spoils to the Convention:

> Most of these persons were still drunk, with the brandy they had swallowed out of chalices . . . Mounting on Asses, which were housed with Priests cloaks, they reined them with Prince stoles.

Carlyle's comment after this quotation from Mercier is: "Man is a born idol-worshipper, *sight*-worshipper, so sensuous-imaginative is he; and also partakes much of the nature of the ape". The radical young American poet, who was "trampled" upon by Lady Eleanore on her arrival to Boston, speaks to her "as reverentially as to a crowned queen, or rather with the awful devotion of a priest doing sacrifice to his idol". This may be a very irreverent comment on Jervase *Helwyse* and American revolutionary fervor when read within the intertextual relation linking the *Legends* to the *French Revolution*. It may also suggest that revolutionary action turns a laudable cause—the opposition to aristocratic pride—into a fateful effect when contaminated by violent deeds; or that the mantle can be seen as interchangeable with the red flag only when a revolutionary action has tainted it.

The loyal party guests try to wrestle Jervase away from the Lady Eleanore and from her mantle. They do so on account of his madness, deeming him, in an echo of Carlyle's image of mad France on the verge of dissolution, a "knave, fool or Bedlamite". Still Jervase frantically presses the silver cup to the lady's lips. Eleanore, scared and aggrieved, wraps herself more closely in her mantle, regardless of Jervase's "new and equally strange petition" that the "accursed" garment should be thrown to the flames in order to gain salvation. The Queen in *The French Revolution*, a woman of pride but still an accomplished and unfortunate Sovereign, confronts the hostile multitudes with a "look of grief and scorn; natural for the Royal Woman" (2, 177), and when seized she, "like Caesar in the Capitol, wrapped her mantle, as it beseems Queens and Sons of Adam to do" (2, 282). It is with a "laugh of scorn" that Hawthorne's character for the second time obsessively wraps herself: "But the Lady Eleanore, with a laugh of scorn, drew the rich folds of the embroidered mantle over her head". The garment becomes the sign of the struggle between revolutionary and loyalist forces. The struggle ends with Jervase's "insane merriment" when he, "impelled by some new fantasy of his insane intellect", snatches the mantle away from the wall of the deserted death chamber of the proud lady, "so worthy to be [its] final victim". Flag and mantle have become one in Jervase's mad actions, and significantly their order is spatially reversed in the end: on his way to his final visit to Lady Eleanore, Jervase snatches first the banner of the plague from the highest portal of the Province-House and then the contaminated mantle. By the power those signs give him he can become the leader of the purifying procession against the pox, but also and more importantly of the historical insurrection. The red flag is seen waving at the end of the tale, while the mantle has already been reduced to ashes. The plague has only apparently been conquered by the burning of Lady Eleanore's mantle, since the sign of its historical effects, the red flag, is brandished triumphantly by the young, demented, American poet when he becomes the leader of the procession that stages the "passing away" of the old power and the liberation of the people.

The flag of the plague has only changed hands, as Eleanore's mantle has been exchanged with the "drapeau rouge" of Carlyle's *French Revolution*. In the exchange a historical transformation has taken place: the 1721 plague inscribed within the text of the French Revolution has become the 1776 Revolution as a plague "whose profound vibrations have not yet ceased to be felt", as Hawthorne wrote in *Septimius Norton*.

The half-obliterated signs of Carlyle's discourse of the French Revolution provide the *Legends* with a "semiotic contact" through which the boundaries of space and time are broken. Carlyle's red "Flag of History" is a haunting presence in the narration of the years 1791-92, while its sign is a haunting presence in Hawthorne's 1721 (or 1776). When the Terror actually breaks out in the chronological sequence of *The French Revolution* (Book Three), its representation turns to phantasmagoric scenes. The invisible banner presides over them, now made present by its effects. Hawthorne's plague symbolically combines a similar chronological anticipation (1721—1775), with the contemplation of the perduring effects of the Revolution. Thus the *Legends* do not stage any action of it, either realistically *à la* Scott, or phantasmagorically *à la* Carlyle, but represent the Revolution through a symbolic displacement (mantle-flag) that discards historiographical sequentiality by uniting anticipation (of the Revolution) and effects (of the plague). Historical events are interchangeable within a symbolic logic. Still, the change is significant. The 1721 plague is like the Revolution, but the event of the 1775 Revolution orients the reader's interpretation of the effects of the plague to those of future past cataclysmic revolutions.

Carlyle's *French Revolution* lends Hawthorne's "Lady Eleanore's Mantle" both symbols and a reader's function. The symbols unify, in their persistence, different historical events; the reader is required, however, to give historical order to these events. Haunting signs from the past are recognizable as signs of a textual memory: the readers' active role is to read through them, to see their effects in reference to their own memory of history, and, eventually, to give them the order of interpretation. To read the American Revolution through the French is in itself a radical attack to contemporary American historiography, engaged in stressing difference. This difference was strongly emphasized, among others, by George Bancroft in his *History of the United States* (whose first volume Hawthorne borrowed on April 3, 1837). Hawthorne, as a reader of Carlyle, sees similarities in disorder; at the same time, the *Legends*, in their entirety, suggest a possible order in the representation of history as phantasmagoria. While Carlyle resorted to the allegory of transcendental Order to contain the revolutionary chaos, Hawthorne suggests the ordering faculties of a modern "historic consciousness", or the ability to reconstruct and possess the past by comprehending its different effects.

THE *LEGENDS* OF THE *PROVINCE-HOUSE* AND THE PHANTASMAGORIC EFFECTS OF SYMBOLS

"In some individual palimpsest", wrote De Quincey, only apparently previous writings have been "displaced" within the sequence of time and genres; some haunting signs have "been regularly called back", "the footsteps of the game pursued . . . in each several chase, have been unlinked, and hunted back through all their doubles" (De Quincey, 1851, 231). The vellum-like property of the individual mind gives order and unity to the seemingly "irrelated and incongruous", "fleeting accidents of man's life and its external shows"

(De Quincey, 1851, 233). The echo of De Quincey's *Suspiria de Profundis* reverberates in Hawthorne's palimpsests of phantasmagoria (*Grimshawe*, 453). De Quincey's subjectivity of vision is deeply rooted in memory. This is a memory activated by the effects produced on the mind by focusing on some momentuous detail of experience.

Henry James commented on *The Legends of the Province-House*:

> Hawthorne had, as regards the two earlier centuries of New England life, that faculty which is called now-a-days the historic consciousness. He never sought to exhibit it on a large scale; he exhibited it indeed on a scale so minute that we must not linger too much upon it. His vision of the past was filled with definite images—images none the less definite that they were concerned with events as shadowy as this dramatic passing away of the last of King George's representatives in his long loyal but finally alienated colony (James, 1967, 74).

Hawthorne's "historic consciousness" is a prominent feature of tales written well before his canonic masterpiece, *The Scarlet Letter* (Lombardo, 1976, 10-11). The modern quality of Hawthorne's "historic consciousness" is, in James's view, characterized by "definite images" of the past; they remain definite even when related to "shadowy" events, and in spite or because of their "minute scale" ("we must not linger too much upon it" warns the disclaiming James). De Quincey's palimpsests and James's "definite images" of the past have in common a focus on their relation to consciousness or vision, the minuteness of their scale, and the awareness of their representative nature.

Reading Hawthorne's *Legends*, James points to "Howe's Masquerade", the first of the four tales, and detects in it the theme ("the passing away" of the Colonial power) which links the separate narratives together. The masquerade introduces this theme by showing a ghostly vision of history, and in the last tale the vision of ghosts evoked by Old Esther Dudley, the symbol of "memory in disguise", duplicates the beginning. Hawthorne's lifelong struggle with a divided loyalty can be read in this "passing" which repeats itself. As Frederick Newberry maintains, Hawthorne could not make himself see the culture of England as "passed"; he was divided, as his "historic consciousness" is, between the political loyalty to progressive and democratic America, and the cultural loyalty to the Old Country (Newberry, 1989). While American historiography recorded the revolutionary event as the realization of a national destiny which excluded the English presence in Colonial America, in the *Legends* Hawthorne writes American revolutionary history recording the persistence of memories which comprehend both insurgent and loyal Americanism. These memories may surface as forgotten details; their presence is "legendary" because excluded from historiography, and "historical" because made visible in the reader's present.

Howe's masquerade is a procession that both "masks" and reveals the imminent end of the British hold on Boston, the first success of the American Revolution. Though many previous instances of Hawthorne's processions come to mind, this procession is distinctly a vision of history: past colonial Governors are seen hurrying out of the Province-House at the strain of a "dead march" and last comes the mask of Sir William Howe. Processions were also a feature in phantasmagoric shows. In *The French Revolution* Carlyle turned into a phantasmagoric representation the actual procession to the church of St Louis of May 4th, 1789; the people as well as the king and the aristocracy were in this procession, marking the first and ineffectual recognition of the Third Estate by the other two. Carlyle's spectatorial narrator focuses on personal gestures and idiosyncrasies, prophetically detecting in them both the forces of the struggle which would soon prove tragically irreconcilable and the actors' fateful part in the scenes that will follow.

Howe himself is a spectator of the procession. His astonishment and rage soon turn into a defiant gesture, and his masked likeness replies by exiting; while doing so,

> he was seen to stamp his foot and shake his clenched hands in the air. It was afterwards affirmed that Sir William Howe had repeated that self-same gesture of rage and sorrow, when, for the last time, and as the last Royal Governor, he passed though the portal of the Province-House (Hawthorne, 1982, 638).

The image of a detail, Howe's gesture, claims the reader's attention. It is a detail contained within a processional masquerade that enacts the past and foresees the future. The reader of both Carlyle's and Hawthorne's processions knows that these prophetic scenes anticipate the actual events to follow. Sir William Howe and his guests do not. Yet the gesture is singled out by them as ominous for their collective future.

In "Old Esther Dudley", Hawthorne represents Howe actually leaving his post, in the tales' unique "staged" episode of the Revolution. The masked anticipation of the procession is here realized for both reader and character:

> With an ominous perception that, as his departing footsteps echoed adown the staircase, the sway of Britain was passing forever from New England, he smote his clenched hand on his brow, and cursed the destiny that had flung the shame of a dismembered empire upon him.

Again two pages later:

> Then Sir William Howe strode forth, smiting his clenched hands together, in the fierce anguish of his spirit (Hawthorne, 1982, 668; 670).

Howe's gesture is an instance of a minute detail from legendary lore turned into a symbol of "the passing away" of the old colonial power. As a symbol it suggests persistence: Sir William Howe's "clenched hands" remain an ominous presence in the collective memory, progressive historiography notwithstanding. As a legendary detail turned into a historical detail, Howe's gesture suggests that a historical field of vision includes seemingly forgotten traces, and "doubles" them, as De Quincey said, in the process of seeing legend (or memory) become history (or reality).

The shift from legends to history is marked by the phantasmagoric effects of seeing the gesture: the gesture is at first presented as half buried, surviving only as gothic fear in the eyes of the fictional beholders. When the legendary detail in "Howe's Masquerade" becomes true to history in "Old Esther Dudley", the last of the *Legends*, Howe's position changes from the historical spectator of an

45

imaginative scene, to the agent in a historical scene. The fictional beholder is old Esther Dudley, the American-born dame who does not fear the future because she believes in the past: she "dwells with memory" and, "if Hope ever seemed to flit around her, still it was Memory in disguise" (670). To her the gesture is not ominous, it stands for an unfortunate fact of history to which she counterposes a rebellious attachment to the past, in the belief that the future is to overturn the present.

Embodying "a history in her person" (671), Esther Dudley mediates between the ghosts of the past and the contemporary reader: she evokes the old colonial governors through a tarnished mirror for the benefit of Boston's children, portrayed as eager spectators of her ghostly visions. Representatives of the past are seen as fearful ghosts only by those who have hurriedly or unconsciously forgotten them. Within the historical setting of the tale—1775 to 1780—the Colonial past cannot plausibly be a memory forgotten by history. The children's parents, the revolutionary citizens of Boston, do not remember, whereas the fearless children are made to see the ghosts as if they were real. The ghosts of Esther's memory belong to the children as "facts" and they retain a pleasant memory of the interaction with the historical apparitions: they "toyed with the embroidery of their rich waistcoats, or roguishly pulled the long curls of their flowing wigs" (673). As new visionary subjects these young implied readers contradict Hancock's revolutionary dictum oriented towards the future: "We are no longer the children of the past" (677). Esther's memory is now their memory, and it is as real as their vision.

The "reality effect" of visions of the past bridges the gap between legends, ghosts, and written history; the reader, as the ultimate onlooker, is "beguiled into believing" that "superstition" is actually true. This was James's opinion, given as further evidence that Hawthorne's romance "rather supplements than contradicts history". "What is created by those images depends on the beholder", writes F. O. Matthiessen, commenting on Clifford's phantasmagoric visions in Maule's well (Matthiessen, 1949, 260). Multiple choice can be the result of such narration; still any choice remains channelled by a narration that casts for the reader a field of vision in which previously separated spheres of experience are shown as contiguous with each other.

In a representation inspired by the analogy between reality and phantasmagoria, signs from the past generate a narration focused on the process of taking in their effects; the narrative sequence is not determined by a cause-and-effect motivation but by repetition with variation of the same sign (Howe's gesture), or by the transformation of one sign into another (mantle—flag). Any "symbolic" narration can be described in these terms; still what concerns us here is Hawthorne's fictional method of writing history. By substituting a process of vision to cause-and-effect sequentiality, Hawthorne's text represents the past as an open-ended interpretation of its effects. While discarding the closure of both progressive historiography and of its literary counter-part, the classic historical novel, his symbolic method complements the open-endedness of the process with the ambition of encompassing all effects produced by the sign elected as representative of the past. To write history has become to write about the visibility of the effects of the past on the present.

Both Michael Colacurcio (1984) and Frederick Newberry (1989) have read the *Legends* as Hawthorne's problematic deconstruction of American historiography of the Revolution. Both critics' analytical methods are determined by the reconstructions of the relation between historiographical sources and their debated significance in Haw-thorne's own time; their interpretation is context-oriented, thus newly historicizing the belief in the supremacy of objective historiographical over imaginative literary methods and truths.

This belief drives their quest for a unity in the *Legends* towards the detection of a hidden, historiographically motivated, cause-and-effect sequentiality between the tales; hence there is in their readings a cer-tain bewilderment at the fact that, though the unifying event is the American Revolution, no episode of it is ever represented "properly", that is, staged in a classic Scott-inspired representation. The *Legends* can be read as new historical fictions, just as Carlyle's *French Revolution* was read in 1837 by John Stuart Mill as a new "poetic" form of historical narration, different both from Scott's historical novels and from the objective historians of his time. Hawthorne patently discards historiographic methods and assesses the ultimate superiority of the "literary" way of telling history by combining subjectivity of vision with the focus on signs from the past previously perceived as belonging to separated fields of experience. At the same time the genre of the historical novel is deconstructed and reconstructed from within. If it is true that a collective textual memory shapes any discourse of history, it is also true that the historical forms of the collective memory are the indivisible part of any process of "writing over".

Sequentiality is a trait shared by historiographical discourse and the discourse of the classic historical novel. A symbolic narration, by contrast, gives a "new order" to events. It is not the order of allegory but, as Jean Normand has pointed out, the order of a "perpetual exchange between the moving changing text of the consciousness and the linear text, milestoned like a road, like a map on the written page" (Normand, 1970, 152). Though the *Legends* are a collection of tales held together by a frame, their sequentiality remains an issue in view of their historical discourse. A sequential cause and effect mechanism can be detected within the order of historical chronology: since "Howe's Masquerade" refers to the last stages of the siege of Boston (1776), "Edward Randolph's Portrait" and the Boston massacre of 1770 can be seen as its cause, the Great Plague of 1721 in "Lady Eleanore's Mantle" as its premonition, Governor Hancock's taking over power in 1780 in "Old Esther Dudley" as the effect of these combined causes. Such renewed sequentiality does not account for the persistence of the representation—regardless of chronological setting—of "the passing away of the old power" in each of the tales; neither does it account for the arbitrariness of combining the reverse chronology of the two central tales (1770; 1721) with the bizarre time contraction between the first and the last tale. The historical time that elapses between the first tale and the beginning of the last is indeed brief, from the last days of the Boston siege to Howe's departure. This time span becomes "legendary" in "Old Esther Dudley", when the old lady is perceived by the now "stern republicans" as the "symbol of a departed system

48

embodying a history in her person", and the four years between Howe's departure and Hancock's arrival are referred to as the "year after year" of a "Memory in disguise".

A "legendary" way of writing history is of course implied by the collective title of the tales and is made verisimilar by their frame telling of old men's fireplace-stories and of an eager young listener in Mr Waite's tavern, once the Colonial Province-House. The Province-House itself is the symbolic space that frames the tales in time. The colonial mansion is the earlier version of the Custom House as a historical public place and of the house of the seven gables as a historical familiar place. It could be described as a compromise between the two, since as a cosy tavern, honored by *habitués*, it is a familiar space; at the same time its old and grand architectural features survive its democratic transformation. By choosing transformation as the vehicle of compromise, the house embodies both old and new. The grandeur of the old is still visible in the new, even if the effects on the narrator as onlooker are uncanny. The presentation of the building if anything intensifies its realistic effects. The change in use of the public structure, not less than the house ghosts, haunt the narrator in his repeated comings and goings. This narrator is Hawthorne's image of the American *flâneur* (Fink, 1990, 11), insistently seen as "entering the arched passage, which penetrated through the middle of a brick row of shops" and transported "in a few steps . . . from the busy heart of modern Boston, into a small secluded courtyard"; and again "diving through the arch way", transported in "a few strides into the densest throng of Washington street". By this "passage", with its "vulgar range of shoe-shops and dry goods stores", the house's ancient "aristocratic front" is hidden but not effaced. The House itself can be read as the image of a modern phantasmagoria, the locus of persistence and transformation, the setting that projects a "passing away" that is not aimed at a resolution in time, but to suggest time in process.

In "Edward Randolph's Portrait", the "legend" following "Howe's Masquerade", Hawthorne provides his reader with a parable on a sign that exposes the limitations of historiographically oriented readings of symbolic narrations. In the second tale of the *Legends*, the Boston Massacre of 1770, commonly considered by historiographers as a cause of the American Revolution, is staged as Hutchinson's drama of divided loyalties. The focus, however, is not so much on the anticipated fratricidal struggle, as on the historian's tragic misunderstanding of a sign of history disguised as a gothic representation. The portrait of Edward Randolph, the colonial enemy of American liberties, develops into a replica of Howe's gesture. Hutchinson is doomed because his historiographical eye cannot make historical sense of an ominous "gothic" perception. He cannot see the anticipation of the coming pre-revolutionary unrest in Edward Randolph's colonial misadventures. The serious mockery of his predicament is intensified by Hutchinson's ostentation of his historical knowledge and expertise: as an historian who carefully investigates the Provincial Records, he claims to have determined, without a shadow of doubt, the real identity of the person portrayed in the blackened canvas and thus dispelled the superstitions surrounding it. While for Hutchinson the portrait is a sign to be read with the method of objective historiography, for everybody else the portrait evokes gothic fears and is "historical" only because part of the house furniture since time immemorial.

There is another implied reader of Edward Randolph's portrait besides Hutchinson—his niece Alice. When Alice's magic Italianate art uncovers the figure portrayed and the accuracy of Hutchinson's historical reading is proved, Hutchinson cannot bear the ominous effect of the picture. Glancing anew at Edward Randolph's likeness, Hutchinson discovers the frightful coexistence of past and present in a sign that he has read only within a system—historiography—that distances characters and events of the past within a beginning and an ending. Alice's art, by contrast, has accomplished the feat of making Edward Randolph visible again. Like Hester Dudley, Alice resurrects the past; and, like Hester Dudley's eager listeners, she believes in legends and in the magic of living memory. Whereas "the children of the past" are "bewildered" spectators, Alice acts as the interpreter of the different effects of seeing the portrait anew. She "sees" in the restored portrait the past in the process of becoming future. The artifact restored by "magic" is finally the sign of a historical future of the past. Alice is the figure of an ideal reader of the *Legends*: she reads the portrait as a palimpsest that contains the persistence of a "stained event". Her interpretation of the gothic effect of Edward Randolph's portrait is that the past may repeat itself; more importantly, her interpretation takes on the form of an anticipatory admonition that, if heeded, will change the "return of the past" into a progressive notion of history. "Behold his punishment—and avoid a crime like his!" cries Alice, addressing Hutchinson (Hawthorne, 1982, 649). Similarly, beholding the images of the past and taking in their effects, Hawthorne's reader is invited to interpret them progressively. In order to do so, Alice and the reader have to accept the notion that progress in time erases neither the presence of the past, nor the visible signs of its memory. The past as eternal return does not deny transformation and progress in Alice's reading. It is the fear of the return of the past which dooms Hutchinson, becomes the "cause" of the Boston Massacre and makes the Boston Massacre symmetrical with both the outbreak of the American Revolution and of the 1721 plague.

Gothic effects in the *Legends* originate in representative signs of the American revolution. Such gothic effects of history make their recipients frenzied to the verge of madness, as happens to Howe, Hutchinson and Jervase. The effects of the red banner are collectively frightful:

> There is no other fear so horrible and unhumanizing as that which makes men dread . . . to grasp the hand of a brother or friend, lest the gripe of the pestilence should clutch him (Hawthorne, 1982, 662).

The collective effect is of a "pernicious" fear. Hawthorne constantly refers to the pernicious effects of the American revolution. In "Old News" (1835) he wrote, "its effects are pernicious to general morality . . . All our impressions, in regard to this period are unpleasant, whether referring to the state of civil society, or to the character of the contest, which, especially when native Americans were opposed to each other, was waged with the deadly hatred of fraternal enemies" (Hawthorne, 1982, 274). A similar statement is made in "The Old Manse" (1846), and again in the later unfinished romances.

The parable of Hutchinson's story shows the cultural uneasiness in the oppositional representation of history—Revolution either in gothic or historiographical modes: nightmarish and historical effects coexist in the canvas the spectators behold, just as they coexisted in the field of vision of the spectators of Revolutionary phantasmagorias. The "gothic" is an effect of objective history, as much as "objective" history has come to be seen through gothic effects. The procession that opens the *Legends* can be seen as a gothic masquerade but it is also a "serious mockery", in the sense of a serious "imitation" of history. Howe's "ominous perception" remains when he finally performs the gesture—turning it into a historical act—in the last legend. His ominous perception now issues from a contemplation of the Revolution and not of its masquerade. Symmetrically, what was perceived as "ominous" by the spectators in the first tale can now be seen as the effect of the revolutionary process. By transferring the ominous effect from the gothic show to the historical scene Hawthorne blurs differences between "imaginative" and "historical" codes of representation: the much discussed opposition between "gothic" and "historical"— originated by Jane Lundblad's classic study (Lundblad, 1947)—is neutralized in a representation that projects as "real" both gothic and historical effects of the same sign.

The coexistence of "gothic" and "historical" accounts for the "characteristic vertigo" of Hawthorne's ghostly visions of history. This "vertigo" brings Scott's method to its extreme consequences. In Scott's sequential, historiographically-authenticated imaginative tales, the literary medium's claim to excellence is supported by its superior inclusiveness. Scott's historical novel, as Lukács pointed out, is the earliest successful example of the bourgeois claim to universality, a first version of a Hegelian "world's prose" (Lukács, 1962). As such Scott's novel would bring together social, anthropological, and psychological motivations and would amalgamate different codes of representation, mainly and broadly defined as historiographical, sentimental, and gothic. Hawthorne's narrative method severs the motivational links, and relies on selected symbols. His own fiction can indeed be read as a process that aims at filling up its self-created gaps,

as Sacvan Bercovitch has shown in his reading of *The Scarlet Letter*
(Bercovitch, 1991). Or, in the words of the narrator of Hawthorne's
Marble Faun, faced with the mystery of "utterances",

> . . . we undertake a task resembling in its perplexity that of gathering
> up and piecing together the fragments of a letter which has been torn
> and scattered to the winds . . . If we insert our own conjectural amend-
> ments, we perhaps give a purport utterly at variance with the true one.
> Yet unless we attempt something in this way, there must remain an
> unsightly gap, and a lack of consciousness and dependence in our nar-
> rative; so that it would arrive at certain inevitable catastrophes without
> due warning of their imminence (Hawthorne, 1983, 929).

This otherwise "unsightly gap" is matched by a new form of continuity, different from Scott's, between codes of representation that are
introduced and amalgamated by substituting motivation with the
subjective interpretation of effects that can coexist with each other.

The different effects that the human eye is capable of perceiving
were described by Brewster as "nicely adjusted" in "the healthy state
of the mind and the body", and, though the visible "creations of
fancy" might have sprung "from a regular series of association", yet he
considered that it was "frequently impossible to discover a single link
in the chain". The sign may be said to be a historically functional
symbol when it shows its capability to elude a motivational chain and
its versatility to change from one place and code to another without
pointing to any prominence of the one in relation to the other.

By stressing a narration of effects Hawthorne enhances the subjective quality of any discourse of history. His post-Scott model could be
said to adjust historical fiction to a notion of modern consciousness,
or to steer its representational value towards a "democratic" aesthetics
of history. The reader, to resume Roy Harvey Pearce's insight, is made
to partake of the process of historical symbol-making, but is also the
recipient and eventually the interpreter of the symbols' effects. A
democratic, middle-class, individual consciousness claims a new universality: in the maze of the effects of the past the reader's action alone
can comprehend them all and discern a "course" of history. Differently
from Lukács's Scott, neither the people nor the nation are the main

concern of Hawthorne's representation of history, but rather the acclaimed American synecdoche, the individual.

As Hayden White has convincingly argued, the modern bourgeois "historic consciousness" was theoretically founded by such historians as Johann Gustav Droysen (1808-1884). His "poetics" of history is for White an early example of a set of principles, both answering the need to see history as organically realized in the present state of society, and devising a "scientific method" out of the intuition that historical narration is a rhetorical, literary act. For Droysen, the historical past "could be known only insofar as it has continued to exist in the present" as "remains" or "sublimations". He instructs historians to make subjectivity, as a modern, dynamic, and all-encompassing entity, the key ideological concern of their rhetorical strategies. Stressing the readers' freedom to choose among the offer of several moral perspectives, the text nonetheless would bind readers to the judgement of their "plausibility". The notion of plausibility is not linked to referential evidence, but to the test of the produced "effects" of historical events seen through the reader's own social and cultural standards. Such contemplation of effects deepens historical understanding—which Droysen considered the aim of historiography, as opposed to Ranke's objectivism—and enables the readers to contain their suppressed fears of the past, thus turning the narration of history into a modern project for contemporary social formation (White, 1987, 83-103). Though Hawthorne as a writer of fiction may or may not have been interested in theories of history, his fictional discourse of history can be seen as a cultural construct that gives shape, in its turn, to a new notion of the order of history.

The need to write history anew was a major concern of his time. "We have a principle—an informing soul—of our own, our democracy . . . this must be the animating spirit of our literature", proclaimed, by no means in isolation, the introduction to the first issue of the *Democratic Review* (Oct. 1837, 1, 1, 14). In this light "history has to be re-written". And history in the September 1839 issue was defined as "the course of civilization", or: "the progress of man from a state of savage individualism to that of an individualism more elevated, moral and refined". This new stage of individualism is matched by the American democratic belief in the rights of the individual man whose "instinctive convictions, . . . irrepressible desires, . . . boundless capacity for improvement" find the ultimate validation both in "the indications of Providence" and in "the teachings of history" (*Democratic Review*, 1839, 6, 211; 213). The *Legends* can be read beyond the irony or the ambiguity of Hawthorne's position as a nostalgic democrat, or tragic conservative. They can be understood as the aesthetic version of contemporary subjectivity faced with the problem of the past; or as fictions whose moral concern is to convey the method through which a more educated, and therefore even radical and iconoclastic, individualism could be achieved. It is a method that would eventually find its disquieting functionality in the office performed by the scarlet letter, as read by Sacvan Bercovitch. As a narration of the past it realizes Emerson's 1836 claim to "an original relation to the universe", re-writing history by focusing on the individual response to it, and by founding a new universality in the beholder's claim of being able to realistically encompass all its effects.

Emerson's 1836 claim to "an original relation to the universe" is followed by a rhetorical question that may evoke Hawthorne's own answer to it in the *Legends*: "Why should we," asks Emerson, setting himself as part of the community of "new men" and "new lands", "put the *living generation into masquerade out of its faded wardrobe?*" (Emerson, 1983, 7; emphasis added). Hawthorne's answer, in its turn, echoes Carlyle's advice to the Concord sage to anchor himself more into the world. "Ideas, Beliefs, Revelations, and such like", wrote Carlyle, and indeed the "whole Past and the whole Future" are embodied in the new man, who is, however, continuous and separate from his generation's "cotton-spinning, dollar hunting, canting and shrieking" (Penn Warren et al., 1973, 16).

A "usable past" can correct the turmoil of the present, or suggest the possibility of a new order; the more so when its notion is formulated within a self-styled culture of the new. As has been remarked, nineteenth-century American fictions are "products of a culture consumed with questions about reconstructing the past", they may be seen as "meditations on the psychological, social, and political effects of viewing specific historical problems as questions on the philosophy of time" (Mizruchi, 1988, 12; 13). In a culture which transforms the representation of history into a meditation on its functioning, even the loathsome colonial past is potentially usable, as the example of the *Legends* may show. Such potential can become a necessity when the signs of the past retain the capability of producing fearful effects on the present. In Hawthorne the question of the usability of the past is left to a reader made aware that the past is "passing", not "passed". Is the past seen in process a "usable" notion for the representation of the exceptional American historical experience and its traumatic discontinuities (migration and Revolution)? This, I think, is the question that Hawthorne's *Legends* project over his major historical fiction, *The Scarlet Letter*, that haunts the "theme of the past" in *The House of the Seven Gables*, and that he finally failed to resolve in the last "aborted" romances.

After *The Scarlet Letter*, Hawthorne attempts only once more, in *The Elixir of Life* manuscripts, to write a "historical romance". He does so by denying the representation of the historical event (the Revolution) that sets Septimius's story in time. On the contrary he claims to intend to focus on an individual consciousness which is possibly "perverted", not only by "senseless" pursuits of eternal continuity, but also by the effects on a mind such as Septimius's of the momentous times of rupture both of his origin and of the Revolution. The representation of history is denied, and the effects of historical events are given as an *a priori* in the individual consciousness. And ultimately the past of Septimius is made unusable by the paradoxical attempt to transform the past into an *eternal* "passing". Does the new notion of the past as "passing", doom rather than redeem the representation of history? It surely dooms older forms of representing history by explicitly marking the shift from represented past to a past "lived" in the present.

The "passing away" of the Colonial power in the *Legends* is referred to "property" claims that historical ruptures have made ambiguous: Howe's gesture, like the land he relinquishes, is both owned by the

American actor who played his part and by himself. Edward Randolph's portrait, the possession of Colonial governors, is now the unacknowledged property of the New England Museum, (possibly, one imagines, hidden in a closet in the room "used in . . . [the] exhibition of the Phantasmagoria"). The Province House itself is downgraded to a tavern in the property of Mr Waite, yet old Esther Dudley still lingers over it as a custodian of the King's right to it. Historical rupture is staged as the struggle over property and power in the snatching of Lady Eleanore's mantle, which changes hands from the proud British aristocrat to the feverish American revolutionary poet, while the snatching of the "flag of history" is ambiguously celebrated in a purifying procession.

When Hawthorne, almost two decades later, was meditating on the palimpsests of phantasmagorias at the breaking point of *Grimshawe*, he was also still debating which criminal deed could have caused the ancestor's migration. In the Etherege version he had determined that whatever the crime, its nature could only be that of property: "It must relate to property; because nothing else survives in this world" (*Etherege*, 287). In his 1844 "Nominalist and Realist" essay, a socially optative Emerson had embellished the Lockean natural relation between property and individual in these terms:

> Money, which represents the prose of life, and which is hardly spoken of in parlors without an apology, is, in its effects and laws, as beautiful as roses. Property keeps the accounts of the world and is always moral. The property will be found where the labor, the wisdom and the virtue have been in nations, in classes and (the whole life time considered, with the compensations) in the individual also (Emerson, 1983, 578).

With the same concern with property and its relations—money, nations, classes, and the individual—Hawthorne's reaction is, almost predictably: "How is it to be particularized & put in action?" (*Etherege*, 287). His failure to find the "how" which can be read in the "aborted" romances strains to the breaking point the symbolic method of the *Legends*. The claim to title and property by the individual as the returning immigrant, self-styled as still suffering from the traumatic break with the land of his ancestors, is repeatedly told as the search for "how" and "why" the passing away of England is still at issue; and as an investigation of the way in which the effects on the mind of the Young American of its main symbol, the bloody footstep on the threshold of a historical estate that is the disputed property between two nations, could be made both comprehensive and plausible for an American reader. Does the "natural" right to property ultimately conflict with a notion of the usable past as "passing", when the "property" can no longer be passed over? Does a representation of the past "lived" in the present need to explore even further the relation between the individual consciousness of the effects of the past and their traumatic consequences on the world of objects? The claim to the past of a returning immigrant may help in "keeping the account" of the American claim to a usable past, by showing the internal struggle of a modern "historic consciousness" facing its divided loyalties.

Part Two

Phantasmagorias, Telegraphs, and the American Claim to the Past

In a moment, in the twinkling of an eye, every act, every design of her past life, lived again, arraying themselves not as a succession, but as part of a coexistence.

—Thomas De Quincey, *Suspiria de Profundis*

That's what your little book says—your little book that's so wonderful for a man uninitiated; by which I venture to mean, you see, a man untravelled. It's apropos of what you call the "backward vision", and I could immediately find the page. "There are particular places where things have happened, places enclosed and ordered and subject to the continuity of life mostly, that seem to put us into communication, and the spell is sometimes made to work by the imposition of hands, if it be patient enough, on an old object or an old surface." It's very wonderful, you know, your having arrived at that, your having guessed it, in *this* place, which denies the old at every turn and contains so few such objects or surfaces.

—Henry James, *The Sense of the Past*

As we cast our eyes over the history of nations we discern with horror the succession of murderous slaughters by which their progress has been marked. As the hunter traces the wild beast, when pursued to his lair by the drops of blood on the earth, so we follow Man, faint, weary, staggering with wounds, through the Black Forest of the Past, which he has reddened with his gore. Oh! Let it not be in the future ages as in those which we now contemplate.

—Charles Sumner, "The True Grandeur of Nations"

A Transatlantic Cable and
The Ancestral Footstep

In the fiction of Hawthorne's unfinished romances, from *The Ancestral Footstep* to *Septimius Felton*, an American makes a claim to an English estate and title, and therefore to recognition as the rightful heir and descendant of an aristocratic lineage which, in one of the versions (*Etherege*), goes back to the Saxons and Normans. The claim has been dormant since the emigration of the first ancestor from England to the New World, and for it to be made effective, the legitimate heir must return to the Old World. The claimant story could be read as the triumphant tale of an imaginary first migrant: the Old World offers him noble origins and a rich estate to crown his colonization of the wilderness, thus bestowing upon that same wilderness the nobility of the oldest Anglo-Saxon past. Yet the reversal of the act of migration could also imply that a successful claim to British property and past would denigrate the American past, by making it merely an episode, not a successful new start in history. The claim to the past once again creates a need for the containment of oppositions: old and new, aristocracy and democracy, disruption and continuity.

Many times it has been said of Hawthorne that he was constantly searching for historical continuity (Newberry, 1989, 202) only to be disappointed, or even appalled by it; that, like Washington Irving and James Fenimore Cooper before him and Mark Twain after him, he was a conservative at heart and a democrat by choice. "If mankind were all intellect, they would be continually changing, so that one age would be entirely unlike another. The great conservative is the heart, which remains the same in all ages . . . ": when this often-quoted notebook entry was written on January 6, 1854, Hawthorne was a representative of his country in the "old home", a consul in Liverpool. He may have been brooding on his own claim to English ancestry; less than four months before in a letter to Fields (Sept. 16, 1853) he had asked his friend to consult an American antiquarian to discover the precise locality from which his ancestor William Hathorne had come. After some unsuccessful attempts, he gave up his quest after a visit to the

61

Record Office where the antiquarian Joseph Hunter told him that "it is very seldom that an American family springing from the earlier settlers, can be satisfactorily traced back to its English ancestry" (*English Notebooks*, 1962, 384). Hawthorne transferred this sentence from the English notebooks to the unfinished romances.

His yearning for continuity might be seen as the impulse behind his vision of himself as the returning immigrant who had left England for the New World two centuries before:

> My ancestor left England in 1635, I return in 1853. I sometimes feel as if I myself had been absent these two hundred and eighteen years— leaving England just emerging from the feudal system, and finding it on the verge of Republicanism. It brings the two far separate points of time very closely together, to view the matter thus (*English Notebooks*, 92).

Such a vision returns again and again in the American's claim to his roots, from *The Ancestral Footstep* to *Grimshawe*. In the texts it allows for the device of a mental time-machine that can present the past as if it were "in action" in the present; at the same time the eerie effects of the presentness of the past, as in a phantasmagoric show, are liable to suggest those differences and subtler connections between the then and the now that would be lost if the past were seen as historically remote.

To a mind like Hawthorne's, as curious about the workings of technological modernity as about those of the past, the desire for a similar subjective contraction of time is metaphorically linked to the telegraph in the first opening pages of *The Ancestral Footstep*. Middleton's wish to solve the riddle of ancestral roots and settle "the heirships of estates" by finding "the past still alive and in action" is supported by the analogy with the telegraph as a means of transmission of his American past onto the past in action he wishes to find in England. The American past and the English past are generally perceived as separate and remote from each other, yet the "riddle" of traditions and family histories whose "solution" is "actually in the world" would not remain such "if only these two parts could be united across the sea, like the wires of an electric telegraph".

Hawthorne's telegraphic analogy at the beginning of *The Ancestral Footstep* can be read within the political debate on the uses of telegraph technology which surrounded the project of the laying of the first Atlantic cable (*French and Italian Notebooks*, 1980, 831). It was a debate that refashioned American identity by figuring anew the relation between the Old and New Worlds and by making a claim to an "imagined community" that would transcend national borders and historical ruptures in the name of common descent.

On both the English and American sides there was great hope for the project's success: after two failed attempts, the cable was hailed as completed in August 1858. For a brief interlude, messages were carried from one shore of the Atlantic to the other; then the current faded out. The Atlantic cable nonetheless played a stirring role in the collective imagination (Melville kept a piece of the cable as a paperweight, which is now on display in the Berkshire Atheneum). The enterprise was seen as an unparalleled application of modern technology and as a "tangible" sign of the renewed bond between England and America. It was a bond that invited a new emphasis on the kinship of the Anglo-Saxon world. The meaning of the telegraph as it was discussed by Congress in 1856—in a debate that ended in March when President Pierce signed the bill on the common English-American enterprise—was informed by both anglophobic and anglophiliac sentiments and parties: the one side enforced the ever present anxiety about the possibility of an Anglo-American war; the other extolled the occasion as one that would end conflict and renew the "brotherhood" of the two countries, the telegraph's "cords of iron" holding them together in "bonds of peace". In July 1857, speaking for England, the Earl of Carlyle echoed the American rhetoric and defined "our new link" as one that far from superseding old yet moral links as race, commerce, friendship, literature, and glory, would give them "a life and intensity which they never had before". To make his meaning plain he went on to suggest that the telegraph, "a strong cord of love", would connect to the Old World "those dear friends and near relatives" who had received "hospitable shelter in America". On August 14, 1857, the day after the failure of the first attempt to lay the cable, Hawthorne recorded a less positive view in his notebook: "In a rail-way carriage two or three days ago, an old merchant made rather a good point of one of the uncomfortable results of electric telegraph . . . since the telegraph had come into play, he . . . may be hit with news of shipwreck, failure, fall of stocks, or whatever disaster, at all hours of the day" (*English Notebooks*, 557).

The Atlantic cable was completed to serve during the Civil War, and even more fervently and urgently was seen at that time, in the words of Mr Seward, as embodying the impatience of the American and English people "to rush into a fraternal embrace which will prove the oblivion of the ages of suspicion, of jealousies and of anger" (Field, 1866). There was a widespread wish that past political dissent, historical ruptures, and present disagreements on momentous issues such as slavery, immigration, and American expansionism would disappear through the magic of that modern connecting link (Crawford, 1987). The land claims and freedom claims dividing the English-American community were at the same time beginning to be balanced against another modern word, Anglo-Saxonism, then emerging in the cultural and political debate in both England and the United States (Higham, 1981; Anderson, 1981). It stood for a brand of nationalism, separate from state boundaries, that defined itself by kinship and descent (Zelinsky, 1988).

Middleton's visit and secret claim to the land of his ancestors links personal identity to political claims, suggesting Hawthorne's involvement with the late 1850s debated meanings of past, race, and national identity, and with the intricacies of re-established brotherhoods and reconstructed common ancestries. Here is the full quotation of Middleton's first declaration of intent:

> "I suppose," said he to the old man, "the settlers in my country may have carried away with them traditions, long since forgotten in this country, *but which* might have an interest and connection, and might even piece out the broken relics of family history, *which* have remained perhaps a mystery for hundreds of years. I can conceive, even, that *this* might sometimes be of importance in settling the heirships of estates; *but which* now, only the two insulated parts of the stories being known,

remain a riddle, *although* the solution of it is actually in the world; *if only* those two parts could be united across the sea, like the wires of an electric telegraph" (*Ancestral Footstep*, 5-6; emphasis added).

Middleton's voice conveys both the wish and the working hypothesis for its realization. The "historical" wish represented by the telegraph is to be tested through a comparative investigation into the meanings of the two legacies, the English and the American. Middleton still sees the two as incommunicable to each other, if not as plainly telling different things. The memories of his family history are disconnected; they survive only as "broken relics", half-buried traces of a "secret" that, once explained, would yield nothing less than a linearity from origin to present and would prove the legitimacy of a unified Anglo-Saxon line of descent. Yet the contorted syntax of Hawthorne's manuscript paragraph, the profusion of adversative clauses which defer or interrupt its discoursive logic, casts a doubtful light on the hypothesis. In the light of doubt, the wish becomes more poignant. Its realization, by contrast, becomes more and more dependent on the overcoming of an epistemological crisis. By sharing the wish of his contemporaries, Middleton is forced both to accept and to question the process that has turned the actual telegraph into a connecting figure in the cultural and political discourse of his time.

The analogy between Middleton's claim and the telegraph both actualizes his quest and, more interestingly, makes it an act of interpretation of the discourse its sign represents. The telegraph is in fact defamiliarized when the metaphor reappears two pages later:

So here was Middleton, now at length seeing indistinctly a thread, to which the thread that he had so long held in his hand—the hereditary thread that ancestor after ancestor had handed down— might seem ready to join in. He felt as if they were the two points of an electric chain, which being joined, an instantaneous effect must follow. Earnestly, as he would have looked forward to this moment (had he in sober reason ever put any real weight on the fantasy in pursuit of which he had wandered so far,) he now, that it actually appeared to be realizing itself, paused with a vague sensation of alarm. The mystery was evidently one of sorrow, if not of crime; and he felt as if that sorrow and crime might not have been annihilated even by being buried, out of human sight and remembrance so long (*Ancestral Footstep*, 8).

"[S]orrow, if not crime": Hawthorne's personal obsession with crime as the repressed or blatantly apparent origin of any story carries with it its unqualified fearful "mystery". By shifting from the process of analogy to its origin—the original "mystery" that the analogy should supposedly overcome—the sign is made to suggest a sinister effect, strongly reminiscent of a Frankenstein-type of electrification which might bring back to life some foul corpse.

This may suggest that the relation between the two elements of the analogy, though necessary in the search for continuity, becomes a threatening or even criminal act of interpretation of reality. It may further suggest that the generalization upon which the analogy has been made is faulty: the two threads of tradition cannot be linked as the cultural rhetoric of the Atlantic cable would suggest, because such unification is based on the generalization of a common origin that is not only historically disputed but textually linked with the mystery of origin and its subsequent qualification as possibly sorrowful or criminal. As further evidence of its faultiness, the "scientific" logic which makes the telegraph a reliable conveyer of messages would itself be denied if its effect were to turn different messages into one. Still, like the vellum of De Quincey's palimpsest, the technology of the telegraph conveys the possibility of a "separate" effort of inscription, and, at the same time, a "writing over".

In *The Ancestral Footstep*, past and present vie with each other in the repeated discussions of the content and usability of traditions. The young American claimant is confronted with an old savior, a Virgil type, who, in Hawthorne's plan, was to be an immigrant who had returned to the land of origin. As the personification of a return, the "palmer" has seen it all, yet he remains a mystery and retains the clue to the mystery of the "ancestral footstep". In the long sections of dialogue Anglo-American traditions are debated, first and foremost the opposition-continuity between the Old and New Worlds, and its related notions, America as the land with no past and America as the unique land of the new. Hawthorne seems to be experimenting with the contemporary *roman à thèse* of writers such as Benjamin Disraeli: the hypothetical thesis, suggested by the various summaries of the projected novel, is that a claim to the past is necessary in order to free the new American of the contradictions of a national identity that discards the past (as passed) while its effects are active in the present.

The solution of the plot is never doubted: once the claim to the past is proved legitimate, the claimant will return to America, materially renouncing title and property. In the projected solution of *The Ancestral Footstep*, a new Adam and a new Eve would become the figures of "a new epoch", the "missionaries of a new social faith", by eating at the tree of knowledge of the past (*Ancestral Footstep*, 58). The "American claimants"—whom Hawthorne had actually met in Liverpool and satirized in his English notebook, and whom he would later portray as a pathetic phenomenon of the age in *Our Old Home* (1863)—would then ideally be transformed into the heirs of all ages.

The projected ending of *The Ancestral Footstep*—never written—was to transmigrate into *The Marble Faun*, with a change of scene and time. For Hawthorne in the late 1850s the past had to be reformed; and for this to occur it had to be seen anew, and in another country. The struggle with a more remote legacy than that of an isolated American past had to become part of the notion of the past, in order for that notion to be "usable" within the construction of a new American identity able to cope with a technological progress that had reduced distances between worlds that were both nationally separated and globally political. A modified version of exceptionalism was required: while the American identity constructed by the revolutionary past relied on oppositions to define difference, this projected American identity would connect the Old and New Worlds and promise to be different because "akin": neither identical nor oppositional.

Recent multicultural developments have familiarized us with similar notions of ethnic pasts of origin and American identity. Their genealogy can be traced back to the nineteenth-century debate on *the* perceived past of origin, the Anglo-Saxon past. The debate on Anglo-Saxonism may be read as a sign of America's postcolonial awareness of being a state whose past originated in the ruptures of the Great Migration and the Revolution, and a nation able to recognize its difference because able to cast "anew" its origin within reconstructed kinships.

It is not within my scope to assess genealogical relations, similarities and differences between Anglo-Saxonism and our contemporary ethnic search for origins: still the project of the American claimant aims at imagining a new historical identity populated, in Benedict Anderson's words, "with ghostly national imaginings" (Anderson, 1983, 17) that cross boundaries of time and space and irresistibly claim their modernity in our postmodern eyes.

MODERN TELEGRAPHY

The Ancestral Footstep is Hawthorne's first attempt at writing an "international novel": the English scene is the setting for the American quest to "solve the riddle" of traditions that have become, in the course of time, disconnected. Strolling in the verdant English landscape, surrounded by signs of the past, Middleton encounters a beautiful young woman, Alice, who blends well into such a landscape. She is, in Hawthorne's project, the New Eve whom Middleton is to marry and take with him to America. Her character appears to descend from the Alice of "Edward Randolph's Portrait" and from the Phoebe of *The House of the Seven Gables*. There is a remarkable difference, however, between the Alice of *The Ancestral Footstep* and her predecessors: like the "palmer", she is apparently English but is an American immigrant returned to England. Already at her first appearance on the narrative scene she is a cultural hybrid or the "natural" medium between two traditions. As the future "heiress of all ages" she is cast as both the depository of the past and the figure of its mediation for the "new".

As Lauren Berlant has recently argued, following Nancy Armstrong's germinal study on desire and domesticity (Armstrong, 1987), the woman's cultural body is the "sphere" of the discourse of national fantasies. Hawthorne's notions of womanhood help to realize the claim of his historical fictions to become vehicles for "proper historic consciousness": as in *The Scarlet Letter* the "female body" is one avenue by which to "realize the contemporary scene that 'receives' cultural transmission" (Berlant, 1991, 37), in the English romances the female body takes on the uncanny power of an untested knowledge.

In *The Ancestral Footstep*, Alice warns the claimant not to pursue his senseless quest into the past and at the same time, inconsistently, spurs him to find out for himself the mysterious something that she knows already. "To what do you allude . . . What object do you suppose me to have?" asks Middleton, trying to fool himself and Alice by calling his quest the innocent amusement of a leisurely tourist—as many Jamesian characters after him would do. Alice persists in returning to the secret quest and declares:

> You have no claim to know what I know, even if it would be an addition to your own knowledge. I shall not, and must not enlighten you. You must burrow for the secret with your own tools, in your own manner, and in a place of your choosing . . . (*Ancestral Footstep*, 12).

Sphinx-like, Alice shifts the topic from the "riddle of traditions" to a method of inquiry. The past can be reconstructed only by an Emersonian individual search; knowledge of it is dependent upon individual means, as it cannot be transmitted, cannot be acquired by addition. Only by testing one's individual potentialities, in one's own way and in a place of one's choice, may one solve riddles. The woman "knows" this much. And what she knows is the only convincing answer to Middleton's own moral dilemma when faced with his wish to connect himself with the past:

> What real right had he—an American, a Republican, disconnected with this country so long, alien from its habits of thought and life, reverencing none of the things which Englishmen reverenced— what right had he to come, with these musty claims from the dim past, to disturb them in the life that belonged to them? (*Ancestral Footstep*, 42).

There is a striking similarity between the character of Alice and that of Aurora in Henry James's *The Sense of the Past*. "[T]he sympathy with Hawthorne is most felt in the last of James's novels", wrote T. S. Eliot

(Eliot, 1969, 161). The similarity between the Claimant manuscripts and James's unfinished novel was noticed by both T.S. Eliot and F. O. Matthiessen and shows in several common "aspects": theme, situations, and technique of presentation. At the outset of both Hawthorne's and James's attempts to write "an international ghost" story—as James called it—the claim to know the past is staged in a dialogue between heroine and hero: the heroine embodies the lived-through experience of another world (Europe), and the hero is setting out for his quest into the past by moving to that world. "The sense of the past *is* your sense", says Aurora as a *viaticum* for her "uninitiated" interlocutor, Ralph Pendrel. The shadow of Hawthorne and his American Claimant manuscripts hovers over Aurora's reference to Ralph Pendrel's "remarkable volume" with a remarkable title: "An Essay in Aid of the Reading of History". Interpreting it for him, she remarks:

> That's what your little book says—your little book that's so wonderful for a man uninitiated; by which I venture to mean, you see, a man untravelled. It's apropos of what you call the "backward vision", and I could immediately find the page. "There are particular places where things have happened, places enclosed and ordered and subject to the continuity of life mostly, that seem to put us into communication, and the spell is sometimes made to work by the imposition of hands, if it be patient enough, on an old object or an old surface." It's very wonderful, you know, your having arrived at that, your having guessed it, in *this* place, which denies the old at every turn and contains so few such objects or surfaces" (James, 1945, 34).

The looked-for "communication" which would yield the individual sense of the past is "sometimes made to work by the imposition of hands . . . on an old object or an old surface". The method of conducting the quest suggested by Aurora, "in aid of the reading of history", is based on an analogy with the curing method of mesmeric or mediumistic trances. And indeed the narration of *The Sense of the Past* is conducted as the narration of a state of consciousness similar to a trance, or as an investigation into the active "superconsciousness" of an observer (Perosa, 1978, 151). James does not fail to modernize it by invoking for his perceiving subject the justification of some sort of "mental illness", thus suggesting a possible reference to his brother's recent investigations on psychic states (W. James, 1986). The writer aims at a "quasi-Turn-of-Screw effect" (294), still the new novel is conceived as a more daring experimentation than the earlier tale; it was to be "expressive of the peculiarly acute Modern", and not "merely apparitional" (Perosa, 1978, 133).

When James set out to write *The Sense of the Past*, presumably in 1899, women's bodies had long acted as vehicles of psychic experimentation. In the 1850s especially their bodies were "telegraphs" connecting the past to the present in mysterious ways, still providing some evidence that messages were carried through. Modern technology functioned as an analogy for the "occult" turned into an experience of the senses: the official weekly of American spiritualism appeared in 1852 with the title *The Spiritual Telegraph*. In 1851 Hawthorne had already employed the analogy in *The House of the Seven Gables*: as Clifford runs away at the unprecedented speed of a train from the old Pyncheon house, his neurotic and modernistic conversation focuses on the telegraph, "an almost spiritual medium", associating it with mesmerism, rapping spirits, psychic energy. The analogy of the telegraph disappears in the versions that follow *The Ancestral Footstep*; its "mediumistic" function however is taken up by the claimant's consciousness: "We shall attach our story to the consciousness of this person, and endeavor to be present with his struggling recollections", Hawthorne writes of his young American Claimant, in an aside in the *Etherege* version (131). Consistently in both *Etherege* and *Grimshawe* the claimant is presented in a state of either wakeful dreams or feverishness, both of which allow the overlapping of past and present, of the American and the English scene, of memories that relate to both personal and collective pasts. In this position of strained perception, the character receives, and attempts to look through, effects produced by agents he does not control. The patent innovation over the *Ancestral Footstep* in *Etherege* and *Grimshawe* is that the quest for a "usable past" is staged from within the—as yet—unexplored functioning of a psychic state.

Hawthorne introduces his attempt to represent his character as "medium" repeatedly and with the same notations, with sentences like "<Make him in a feverish dream, that shall mix itself with the scene>" (132); "<Etherege lies in a dreamy state, thinking fantastically, as if he were one of the Seven Sleepers> <He does not open his eyes but lies there in a maze" (307); "<Describe him as delirious, and the scene is adopted into his delirium" (451). And again, this time introducing the paragraph quoted at the beginning of my discussion of phantasmagorias: "<Make this whole scene very dreamlike and feverish>" (453). The claimant is "magnetized" by the English ancestral mansion, which is both ancient and new: "a modern mansion built upon the foundation and taking in some of the walls of an old castle", Hawthorne writes in one of his "studies" (476). To Etherege,

> the mansion itself was like dark-colored experience, the reality; the point of view where things were seen in their true lights; the true world, all outside of which was delusion, had here—dream like as it sometimes seemed—the absolute truth (*Etherege*, 299).

The phantasmagoric scene of the represented world should mix itself with the focus on deranged yet preternaturally active states of perception that would lend authenticity to the dream because of the state of the "dreamer".

The claimant may appear as an alter ego of Hawthorne's ghostly genius described in 1864 by Richard Holt Hutton as that of "a man who consciously *telegraphed*, as it were with the world, transmitting meagre messages through his material organization" (*Spectator*, July 18, 1864). In a similar light Henry James may have read Hawthorne's aborted romances in writing *The Sense of the Past*. This is a novel, T.S. Eliot wrote, in which one may "detect Hawthorne coming to a mediumistic existence again, to remind a younger and incredulous generation of what he really was" (Eliot, 1969, 163).

Recent readers of the American Claimant manuscripts have reversed Davidson's verdict that the unfinished romances are an instance of Hawthorne's failing creative powers (Davidson, 1949) by stressing their experimental quality (Newberry, 1989; Swann, 1991; for an opposite view: Brodhead, 1986). Gloria Erlich considers the romances an attempt at a "psychological study truly remarkable for its time" (Erlich, 1984, 151). Erlich's reading opposes Frederick Crews's dismissal of them as a "step backward" in Hawthorne's work of "psychological truth". In his bio-psychoanalytic orientation Crews misses the experimental "psychic" quality of the romances, going so far as to state that in "his last romances Hawthorne wanted to produce agreeable plots without suffering the emotional strain increasingly apparent in the three preceding romances" (Crews, 1966, 245). My contention is that in developing the first draft (*The Ancestral Footstep*) into the second and the third (*Etherege* and *Grimshawe*) Hawthorne attempts to frame the claim to an English estate, and its attending symbol, the ancestral footstep, into a narration of inward states of consciousness that, far from being "a step backward", carries further his own claim to the representation of a modern historic consciousness.

As Berlant suggests, by the time he wrote *The Scarlet Letter*, Hawthorne had already come to see "the past as a problem for modernity" to be "inscribed" in the subject. The "authenticity" of a representation of the past—or its verisimilar notion—is consequently founded on "emotional, affective psychological sovereignty" (Berlant, 1991, 148). Still such "authenticity" is a notion that has to be rethought "historically", as Joel Pfister maintains; Hawthorne's "psychological truth" should be seen "in the framework of the social construction of psychological codes and the emergence of the 'psychological' as a category produced within the middle-class" (Pfister, 1991, 17). Psychological authenticity can be measured through notions of gender, as it is by both Pfister and Berlant; still, such notions are intricately connected to the developing notions of the psychic workings of the human mind of the 1840s and 1850s, as is made apparent by even a cursory glance at the debate on mesmerism and related "sciences", and at Hawthorne's own personal and fictional involvement within this debate.

As a preliminary step to the analysis of Etherege's "feverish states" let us start from the apparent contradiction in Hawthorne's metaphorical use of human electricity, in the belief that it reveals a notion of identity related to the cultural debate on mesmerism. The analogy to electricity is textually applied both to the normal, active, socially functioning body and to deranged mental states. The claimant's derangement is rewritten in the *Grimshawe* version both with a direct reference to "the unknown laws that govern such psychic states" (450) and with a resumption of the "electric wires" metaphor: "the electric wires, that had connected him with the battery of life, were broken for the time, and he did not feel the unquiet influence that kept everybody else in galvanic action" (458). The reversal of the analogy from alluding to nervous states to alluding to "normal" functional reality is only apparent; both body and mind activities were "scientifically" described in connection with the "electric fluid theory".

Mesmerism founded its claims to a "science of the mind", "by postulating an identity between the human nervous system and the magnetic medium now "known" to transmit sensations in the material universe" (Fuller, 1982, 59). "Let us establish the fact", wrote the eminent mesmerist John Bovee Dods, summarizing a long debate, "that electricity is, indeed, the *connecting link* between mind and body" (Dods, 1850, 55). In a world defined as an electromagnetic field only waiting to be activated, wires understandably become "nerves", and vice versa. In *The House of the Seven Gables*, Clifford says: "The world of matter has become a great nerve, vibrating thousands of miles in a breathless point of time? Rather the round globe is a vast head, a brain, instinct with intelligence" (Hawthorne, 1983, 578). It is not difficult for his interlocutor, the old gentleman as implied reader, to decode Clifford's allusion and bring it back to earth, to the modern Morse telegraph and to contemporary social, economic, and political issues. Morse himself had described his invention in revolutionary social terms that borrowed from physiology their suggestive explanation:

> it is not visionary to suppose that it would not be long ere the whole surface of this country would be channelled for those nerves which are to diffuse, with the speed of thought, a knowledge of all that is occur-

ring throughout in the land, making, in fact, one neighbourhood of the whole country (Bush, 1977, 93).

The most significant cultural innovation of the telegraph, as Clive Bush has commented, regarding the above quotation, "is the externalization of the nervous system into a total field of interplaying information as electric strains" (Bush, 1977, 94). The "mind" spreads its tantalizing power over space and time, the political and social body, so that the individual mind can acquire the status of the first and foremost shaper of a world where telegraphy provides a realistic analogue.

As Taylor Stoehr has convincingly argued, Hawthorne's scientific interests reflected the combination of "pseudosciences" of the mind and social sciences of his own time (Stoehr, 1978). Mesmerism and philanthropy together worked toward the realization of a utopic democratic "mastermind" that by exploring physical facts would lead to a better social functioning, or that by explaining social functioning with physiological analogies would contribute to further consensus and shape national identity.

Brewster's *Letters on Natural Magic* explained "animal magnetism" as a mind function whose potentialities were as yet unexplored, and mesmeric treatises focused on physiology to explain "mediumistic phenomena". John Dods added to his 1843 *The Philosophy of Mesmerism* the more modern-sounding, *The Philosophy of Electrical Psychology* (1850), or the doctrine of electric "impressions". Extolling electricity as the common frame of reference of the physiology of body and mind made the mind, by implication, figure as a function of the body. The unknown laws of psychic states were explained by Dods as the effects of positive and negative poles, equally responsible for man's actions and movements and for nervous derangements. When movement of the body is eliminated, as in illness, a larger amount of energy flows to the mind, enhancing its function and possibly serving as a healing factor; so Stanley Grimes maintained in his widely influential and controversial *Etherology* (1850)—it is too tempting not to suggest a resemblance between Grimes's title and the claimant's name,

75

Etherege. Grimes also calls the function performed by the mind "consciousness" and locates it in the "medulla oblongata" of the brain: "this is the point where sensation terminates, and volition commences" (Grimes, 1850, 101). Both voluntary and involuntary impulses are received by this portion of the brain, and a functioning consciousness is able to connect them by the exercise of the "reflective powers", upon which conscious memory especially depends (115).

As Henry Ellenberger has shown, the notion of a "dual model of the mind with a conscious and unconscious ego" began to be developed by the nineteenth-century followers of Mesmer (1970, vii). The debate that would lead to the secularization of the mind and turn it into the modern notion of psyche was open. Thus, in 1857 the Harvard Divinity School was still called to investigate the existence of spiritual telegraphy which it denied; at the end of the century, Professor William James's research on mediums and hypnotic states led to the notion of the division of "consciousness", according to which a part of the subject acts as a spectator and critic of the performance directed by the other part (W. James, 1981, 204-9).

In a formulation that resembles William James's, for Grimes the very notion of identity descends from the proper functioning of the reflective powers of consciousness, since "Identity is an idea that I am the *same* person that I was, and this is certainly a notion which can only arise upon Comparison and Connection, or Causality" (Grimes, 1850, 141). When such reflective powers are suspended there is a disturbance in the "connecting link" (the electric fluid); or as John Dods put it, the "nerves, like so many telegraphic wires" throw out of balance "the electricity of the system" (Dods, 1850, 71), and both "mental" and "physical" impressions are not channelled into controlled action but become disturbances, psychic and physical.

While striving to give scientific foundation to mesmerism, Chauncy Townshend, in his *Facts on Mesmerism* (1844), dismissed "animal magnetism" and invited scientific research to concentrate on a unique state of consciousness, whose conditions and properties should be investigated in their own right (Fuller, 1982, 40). In 1854 Townshend published a refutation of mesmerism's critics, disclaiming physiological analogies and admitting that "the wonders of our sentient being are only *beginning* to be scrutinized". The analogy he draws upon for the new science is now astronomy (and evokes Hawthorne's Septimius Felton's rational justification for his alchemical pursuit):

> our astronomers, I say, are pursuing that problem [the revolution of the sidereal system] not for themselves, but for another generation. That mighty legacy must they bequeath to the extended investigation of their children, or their children's children; for one life is inadequate to ascertain or to compute even one segment of the mighty circle . . . How shall then we presume prematurely to give [psychic phenomena] that fixity which shall circumscribe their further development, and limit us in their progressive investigation and comprehension? (Townshend, 1854, 38).

The investigation of psychic states is featured as the most daring of sciences, and requires to be recognized as a "specific" area of inquiry. Townshend goes so far as to postulate the patient's physical reality as determined by his own "mesmeric" or nervous energy: the ways in which this is achieved are still "a puzzling residuum"; yet evidence suggests that in a psychic state perceptions are accrued by a "transposition of the senses" by which curing "visions" emerge. The same view was held by James Braid, the British physiologist who ennobled mesmeric phenomena by giving them the name "hypnosis" (*Neurohypnology, or the Rationale of Nervous Sleep Considered in Relation with Animal Magnetism,* 1841).

Though Hawthorne was, on spiritual grounds, adverse to the "mesmeric cure" of Sophia Peabody in 1841, his interest in animal magnetism and mesmerism is documented (Stoehr, 1978) and rendered many times in his work from the early "Alice Doane's Appeal" to the later *House of the Seven Gables* and *Blithedale Romance.* In London in 1857 Hawthorne discussed mediumistic writing with doctor Wilkinson, and in Florence in 1858—at the time he abandoned *The Ancestral Footstep* for *The Marble Faun*—he was exposed to the "psychic" beliefs of the Brownings. In Florence he also witnessed a seance during which Sophia "communicated" with her dead mother. The entry in Hawthorne's journal recording the event reads:

> The matter seems to me a sort of dreaming awake, my wife being, in the present instance, the principal dreamer. It resembles a dream, in that the whole material is, from the first, in the dreamer's mind, though concealed at various depths beneath the surface . . .

There is a "lurking skepticism" of the "occult" in Hawthorne's view; he believes, however, in the reality of effects produced by the mind. He ends his entry lamenting the "pig-headedness both of metaphysicians and physiologists in not accepting the phenomena so far as to make them the subject of investigation" (*French and Italian Notebooks*, 1980, 399-400).

Tellingly, the "sense of unreality" to be investigated is metaphorically rendered by "the most vivid phantasmagoria of a dream". Hawthorne, as James Mellow suggests, "could neither believe nor disbelieve" (Mellow, 1980, 506) in psychic phenomena. Still, when in 1860 he returns to his American Claimant story, the wish to find the past "alive and in action" yields a method of representation that focuses on psychic states as a time-machine that "electrifies" the past into the present.

Emersonian national imagination considered building "the sepulchres of the fathers" harmful. Nonetheless these are sepulchres that cannot be denied. They live on in the collective imagination: can the new technology of the mind account for their persistence, while progressive enthusiasms cast them as overcome? To leave the past alone has become a conservative answer to the issues aroused by the representation of a "modern" consciousness. Technology of communication electrifies space and time in new continuities; similarly a technology of the mind is struggling to "naturalize" in a new scientific system the still "occult" perception that the past survives in the present. Hawthorne's attempt to focus on the American Claimant's psychic states provides evidence for a radical notion of the present in which the past strives to become "pragmatically" real in new forms.

THE PHANTASMAGORIA OF NATIONAL MEMORY:
ETHEREGE AND *GRIMSHAWE*

In the interior recesses of the magnetic English mansion, Hawthorne writes in *Etherege*, abruptly shifting to the first person singular:

> There is—or there was, now many years ago, and a few years also, it was still extant—a chamber, which when I think of, it seems to me like entering a deep recess of my consciousness, a deep cave of my nature . . . (*Etherege*, 335-6).

Similarly, the magnetized claimant feels as if "underneath this manor house were the entrance to the cave of Trophonius; one visit to which made man sad forever". "Caves" are of course favorite repositories for Hawthorne's "heart". This particular instance shares with De Quincey's *Confessions* an analogy with Trophonius's cave as the impervious locus of divination. It is the cave where the treasure is buried, the same treasure that the architect Trophonius coveted to the point of killing his brother. Either in punishment or in horror he never leaves the cavern alive and becomes an oracle whose divinations require a particular ritual of the supplicant. The supplicant has first to forget his past by drinking at the spring of Lethe, and then drink of the Water of Memory in order to be able to remember. He is then ready to listen. Once the oracle has finished speaking, the supplicant loses all sense and understanding; in this state he emerges from Trophonius's deep chasm and is enthroned in the Chair of Memory, from which, by his medium, the oracle is delivered. Only after such delivery does the supplicant recover his senses and become able to return to the House of Good Genius and be happy again (Graves, 1955, 179-80).

Trophonius's cave and its rituals serve as the mythical analogy for a modern process of forgetting and remembering. Descending into Trophonius's cave, as the American Claimant is said here to have attempted to do, may be Hell: "I wish the Devil had kept him there!" says Hawthorne in one of his humorous asides. Still, such descent, once tried, can transform a common man into a morally valuable individual: "It seemed, whatever it might be, to have converted an ordinary superficial man of the world into a being that felt and suffered inwardly, had pangs, fears, a conscience, a sense of unseen things" (*Etherege*, 299). The process through which the young American reaches back into the past can in itself have a redeeming quality that may atone for possible crimes of the past whose evil effects endure in the present.

In a world perceived as a phantasmagoria memories of the past surface unexpectedly. The past is "still alive and in action" in Thomas De Quincey's romantic subjectivity. De Quincey alludes to the telegraph when, in *The Suspiria de Profundis*, he poetically explains the function of memory as an analogy-making process that bridges the gap between traumatic childhood memories and adult sentient experiences:

> . . . amongst my mortifications have been compliments to my memory, when in fact any compliment that I merited was due to the higher faculty of an electric aptitude for seizing analogies, and by those aerial pontoons passing over like lightening from one topic to another . . .
>
> This being so, it was no great instance of that power, that three separate passages in the funeral service . . . restored themselves perfectly when I was lying awake in bed . . . (De Quincey, 1851, 192-3).

When describing the conscious taking hold of memories, of those "mighty phantoms" that randomly surface from the deep, "hieroglyphics written on the tablet of the brain" which "disdain the infirmities of language", the function of the experiencing subject is that of a medium able to translate into words their mysterious presences:

> *They* wheeled in mazes; *I* spelled the steps. *They* telegraphed from afar; *I* read the signals. *They* conspired together and on the mirrors of darkness *my* eye traced the plots. *Theirs* were the symbols; *mine* are the words (241).

De Quincey's romantic subjectivity fostered, as George Poulet has shown, a new concept of time totality in the simultaneous experience of past memories and present perceptions that inaugurates the tradition of Marcel Proust's *Remembrance of Things Past*. It is the same concept that Baudelaire developed in his 1857 abridged translation-commentary of the *Confessions*, reading the horror as well as the promise in the conviction that in the palimpsestic human brain or consciousness nothing is ever forgotten (Poulet, 1968, 4, 182-92). As Hawthorne puts it in *Etherege*:

> it is very curious to see what turnings up there are in this world of old circumstances that seemed buried forever; how things come back, like echoes that have rolled away among the hills and been seemingly hushed forever. We cannot tell when a thing is really dead; it comes to life, perhaps in its old shape, perhaps in a new unexpected one; so that nothing really vanishes from the world. I wish it did (*Etherege*, 284).

The past is not passed: the theme is the same as that of *The House of the Seven Gables*; the suspicion that something is still amiss in its treatment can be read in Hawthorne's tortured asides. One of them is both a denial and a reminder of the old man Pyncheon's story: "How can it appear as if dead men's business, that had been buried with them, came to life again, and had to be finished now? Truly this is hard;—here is the rub; and yet without it the story is meagre and barren" (*Etherege*, 198). And "medium" is another torturing keyword in Hawthorne's asides: it applies both to a sense of identity and to a "neutral ground" where mysterious signs struggle to become conscious realities. "There is no medium in my life between the most vulgar realities, and the most vaporous fictions", Etherege says of himself (260).

For Baudelaire, when space is magnified and time is expanded, temporal and spatial distance annihilated, the subject has to face "le terrible compte-rendu des toutes ses pensées terrestres" (Baudelaire, 1976, 184); the memory of evil upsets the positive implication of the technological metaphor of the telegraph. Though it may appear a trivial detail, the telegraph metaphor in De Quincey's text is not "translated" by Baudelaire. Hawthorne clings, by contrast, to potentially positive implications of the telegraph analogy. His claimant, like De Quincey's self, attempts to "read the signals" "telegraphed from afar", hoping to overcome the memory of a possible guilt in the presence of a bloody footstep in the past of origin.

Hawthorne's "neutral ground" is refashioned as depending upon an "internal ground", as a psychic state in between dream and reality. In his feverish yet wakeful states the claimant willingly yields to the surging of memories:

> When he awoke, or began to awake he lay for some time in a maze, not a disagreeable one, but the thoughts were running to and fro in his mind, all mixed and jumbled together. Reminiscences of early days, even those that were pre-Adamite; referring we mean, to those times in the almshouse, which he could not at ordinary times remember at all, but now there seemed to be visions of old women and men, and pallid girls, and little boys that could be referred only to that epoch. Also, and most vividly, there was the old Doctor, with his sternness, his fierceness, his mystery; and all that happened since, playing phantasmagoria before his yet closed eyes; nor, so mystified was his state, did he know, when he should unclose those lids, where he should find himself. He was content to let the world go on in this way, as long as it would, and therefore did not hurry, but rather kept back the process of awakening; willing to look at the scenes that were unrolling for his amusement, as it seemed; and willing too, to keep it uncertain whether he were not back in America, and in his boyhood, and all other subsequent impressions a dream or a prophetic vision (*Etherege*, 308).

The narrative focus is on the dynamic formation of memories as both willing and unwilling impulses that reach into the sphere of conscious "reflective powers". The field of vision is shaped by the character's willingness to keep the involuntary images of memories, the half-buried images of the past, within his sentient consciousness: childhood memories, deeply buried, "pre-Adamite", not ordinarily remembered, are willingly retained for contemplation.

Such willingness suggests the pleasure of a regression that allows a forgotten, and even unpleasant, past to come alive. It also suggests the desirability of a condensation of space and time. The images from the past are of a New World childhood contemplated anew in the Old. The displacement in space allows for a contraction in time: all the other "impressions" since childhood are displaced by the conscious "reflective power" into a vague, yet potentially present, "dream or a prophetic vision" that expands ad infinitum the chronological time of the character's life and, by implication, of the national time of young America. Contradictions and ruptures are erased by blissful correspondences in the character's consciousness.

A noise apparently interrupts Etherege's willing "daydreaming". Only apparently, though: seeing with his open eyes another person—an aged man, the palmer—in the room, he is impelled to "see" "the old family personified". This time the involuntary surging of memory shifts the content from childhood to "legend". It is the "old family legend" that appears in Etherege's field of vision: he has seen the very "demon of the house", and its effect is of "shadowy terror". Etherege's reflective powers recoil for a moment: "Where am I?" he now asks. "What are you?" (311; 312). Applying himself to reflect on his "legendary" memory turned real in his frightful perception of the old man, Etherege resorts to the mythic history of an English past of origin to dispel his terror: the old man, in "extreme age", when "the nineteenth century was elderly", is transformed into "a being that might have been young when those old Saxon timbers were put together, with the oaks that were saplings when Caesar landed; and was in his maturity when the Conqueror came" (311).

Etherege is willing to overcome his terror in the recognition of a mythic past of origin. Still, if the past of origin is "still alive and in action", then, he cries out, "Where was America and the Republic in which he hoped for such great things?" (309). The "shadowy terror" is now consciously seen as the effect of the willing erasure of an intervening past, from childhood to youth, from Anglo-Saxon origins to Republican America. Does his vision erase national memory, or does the vision of a mythic past of origin lend continuity to history in a new ahistorical, kinship-based notion of national memory?

Both the fear of erasing history and the desire for continuity are made "authentic" within Etherege's psychic state. While lingering on childhood memories he prefigures the intervening past as "a dream or a prophetic vision". That same intervening past is subsequently perceived with the horror of a historical absence. Dreamy states bring no fear: the images of his American childhood are fondly contemplated in the English space: "In the dreamy state, he felt no fear": England as the World of the Old and America as the World of the New— Adamite, young, mythically progressive—may coexist as pleasant overlapping presences. But "as a waking man, it was fearful to discover that the shadowy forms did not fly from his awakening eyes". Still, as befits a Young American, Etherege struggles to keep hold of himself, of his place in history, among "shadowy forms": in his second attempt to overcome the fear caused by his perception of shifting forms, his "neutral ground" of vision is enlarged to include pragmatic evidence:

> Etherege could not bear the awe that filled him, while he kept at a distance, and coming desperately forward, he stood close to the old figure; he touched his robe, to see if it were real; he laid his hand upon the withered hand that held the staff, in which he now recognized the very staff of the Doctor's legend. His fingers touched a real hand, though, bony and dry, as if it had been in the grave.
>
> "Then you are real?" said Etherege doubtfully (313).

Etherege's visions are made verisimilar by the tested "reality" of memories. Touching a real hand proves their "authenticity": the staff is the "very staff of the Doctor's legend", one object which connects Etherege's childhood memory of his legendary and traumatic English origin with the presence in contemporary England of a form whose "reality" he had at first only ascribed to his dreamy state. Is the old man "real" because of the recognized legendary memory of the "old staff", or because he is endowed with a concrete hand? Etherege's question—"Then you are real?"—can be answered in both ways: in the phantasmagoria of the psychic state palimpsestic memories of the past keep surfacing and prove to be as real as the evidence of the senses.

Showing the reconstruction of the dynamic relation between memory and immediate experience "as it happens", within the reflective process of a character, the text shows as well the possibility of a discourse that may contain the effects of the experience of a new "reality", the copresence of the desire for a past of origin, and the fear of historical erasure. In such mediumistic discourse, *any* memory of the past is potentially active and "visible" in the present. Memories of guilt and memories of hope can be shown as contiguous with each other. At the same time the surfacing of the individual memories in the claimant's consciousness dramatizes the contiguity of national dreams and fears. Etherege's memories clash with his reflective powers when "their shifting forms" clash with republican collective memory and its notion of national past as progressive revolutionary erasure:

> The moral, if any moral were to be gathered from these paltry and wretched circumstances, was, "Let the past alone: do not seek to renew it; press on to higher and better things—at all events to other things; and be assured that the right way can never be that which leads you back to the identical shapes that you long ago left behind. Onward, onward, onward!" (*Ancestral Footstep*, 56)

This resembles the "moral" of American accounts of the national past; it is a historical imperative lifted almost verbatim from Hawthorne's English notebook (*English Notebooks*, 488-9) and one that had previously appeared as the belief of Young Americans such as Holgrave and Miles Coverdale. In the last legend of the Province-House the "moral" is given a historical origin in the words of Governor Hancock when taking over Howe's post as the representative of the new Republic:

> "She hath done her office!" said Hancock solemnly. "We will follow her reverently to the tomb of her ancestors; and then, my fellow-citizens, onward—onward! We are no longer the children of the Past!" (Hawthorne, 1982, 677).

The office of Esther Dudley, the "symbol of memory in disguise", is said to be "done" by him who represents the victory of the American Revolution. Yet the "reality effect" of such office survives in the children to whom old Esther told her "legends". In the *Legends*, the children are the recipients of someone else's memory; in *Etherege* and *Grimshawe* memory is represented in action within an individual consciousness. The focus on psychic states becomes the testing ground for the continuity between "legendary" memory and experience, between past and present and the two geographical spaces that represent them. Old Esther Dudley needed a "tarnished mirror" to make the past come

85

alive: now the mirror symbolism disappears or is literalized in recurrent "waking dreams" that assess the reality of the past in the present. The implications of Etherege's represented "daydreaming" are manifold: within Hawthorne's canon they carry to the extreme consequence the method of romance; within the tradition of fictions of the past, the way is opened for the replacement of a represented past by a represented self in the process of "taking in" the past; within the formation of the notion of a "usable past" in Hawthorne's own culture, the morally progressive imperative (onward!) becomes true only when it means to "see" the past in process within the forms of the new.

Etherege is a foundling and Hawthorne does not reconstruct the mystery of his birth; as a foundling, however, he is adopted by an English immigrant doctor—a vengeful character reminiscent of Godwin's and Brockden Brown's enlightened and evil superheroes. The Doctor is surrounded by spiders and spiderwebs which represent both his scientific endeavor and the mysterious plot he weaves for the boy's destiny. From the boy's early childhood, the Doctor weaves for him the myth of an aristocratic English origin, which, when time comes, is to turn the foundling into a claimant. Still, while claiming his home and origin in the Old World, Etherege is a successful democratic young man engaged in working out an identity for himself that might become nationally representative. He is an "American rambling about in quest of his country" (*Etherege*, 221) in the very locus of the past. In England he finds a substitute for oppositional geographical and historical "realities" in the reality of his own mind forged both by a myth of origin and by a myth of progress. The workings of the claimant's mind cast out the notion that American identity is dependent on the recognition of a national "psyche" which nourishes the desire of each individual to be both the ancestor and the descendant.

When the claimant is not feverish in bed, recovering from his wound, he "wanders" around. He is the *flâneur* in the English countryside, a man of leisure, who, Hawthorne decides, should have conferred upon him the distinction of being the official Ambassador of his country. Jamesian ambassadors come irresistibly to mind, and their genealogy appears to be grounded within Hawthorne's representation of a claimant to an English past of origin. It is a past perceived through visions of an American eye contemplating "anew" the English scene, or contemplating the effects of a scene that has been transmitted, in American culture, as the scene of the old. "Taking in" such a scene is taking it in "anew" because of the representation of an inward process that in itself proves the moral value of the individual.

The nationally acclaimed death of the past is a devious claim, to be, by all means, corrected: the solution may lie in choosing a time and place as the origin of one's American self, as recent quests for ethnic roots have made manifest. For Anglo-Saxon, post-revolutionary Hawthorne the quest was naturally connected to England; still, with his claimant Hawthorne envisions a paradigm for future development of pluralistic continuities: each individual can construct an ethnic origin in an imagined past and place and make such origin compatible with national homogeneity, within the overall progressive category of Americanism.

Seeing anew—not seeing for the first time—is a constant paradigm of the claimant's contemplation of the English scene. Over and over the "awakening to a former reality" (148) is seen "yet with a newness" (168) through the protagonist's senses: "heaps of new things, new customs, new institutions" make the past "seem" dead. Still:

> his return had seemed to dissolve away all this incrustation, and the old
> English nature awoke all fresh, so that he saw the green grass, the
> hedgerows, the old structures and old manners, the old clouds, the old
> rain-drops, with a recognition and yet with a newness (*Etherege*, 168).

In *Etherege*, Holgrave's metaphor of the young giant carrying about the corpse of the old giant—"Shall we ever get rid of the Past? . . . It lies upon the present like a giant's dead body . . . and only needs to be decently buried" (Hawthorne, 1983, 509)—is repeated with a difference: the past which hangs "like a millstone round the country's neck, or incrusted in stony layers over the living form; so that to all intents and purposes, it is dead" (*Etherege*, 165) is the English past in England, and it is "dead" for the English. A new interpreter of its presence has materialized in the American Claimant. Consequently the past is shown in the process through which it is "disencrusted". The ideological "onward" is not dismissed in *Etherege* and *Grimshawe* but seen within a process of going "backward" that compares and attempts to connect: in the process the claimant's present is "renewed" by the past. "Onward" is not oppositional to "backward" but contains it with a difference: "Age is our novelty", as Etherege says, "therefore it attracts and absorbs us", and an English old house may appear to have a "charm" for this young American that is "like the freshness of Paradise" (*Etherege*, 148; 168).

Hawthorne's claimants and James's passionate pilgrims may see the land of the past for the first time, yet they see it with a foreknowledge that is to be reformulated by their "reflecting powers". Be it a foreknowledge of disconnected threads of a family legend; or documents suggesting the legitimacy of heirships lost in time; or more "realistically" the result of the reading of histories, guidebooks, or manuals for the leisured tourist, it is a foreknowledge that may be activated as a "paramnesic" memory that sees afresh the New World in the Old, or brings the Old World back within the conscience of the New.

Such foreknowledge may however become puzzling when one is confronted with "the real thing", as both Hawthorne's claimant and James's Ralph Pendrel could testify. It can take the shape of upsetting yet terribly fascinating mediumistic phenomena, when seeing "anew" means seeing things that refuse to be recognized as personal memories. In fact the most upsetting and the most investigated phenomenon of mediumistic trances was the relation between memories that the medium might have actually stored, and "memories" that apparently did not belong to the medium's individual experience, but that somehow surfaced in his consciousness.

William James, though convinced of the existence of such phenomena, did not solve the problem. In Hawthorne's time the "electric fluid theory" would connect such puzzling "residuum" to the universe as the ultimate electric field. Through "suggestion" natural to the subject or artificially induced by the mesmerizer, loose electrical impulses would take the form of a pre-knowledge (clairvoyance) or an after-knowledge (communication with the past or its "spirits"). To prove the independence of the nervous system from "magnetic" fields, Townshend cites the evidence of cases where the subject "beholds . . . what was never suggested" (Townshend, 1854, 170). The "natural" power of nerves to make the subject "see" things and events of which she or he has no previous knowledge is undeniable, Townshend maintains, and is even more striking when the content of vision refers to something which is "distant" in space and time from the perceiving subject. What is "seen" is seen for the first time "here and now", but it happened in another place and in another time. There is no "sleight of the eye", Townshend insists, in these experiments; it is not a matter of seeing "through a mirror" but of "literally seeing it, and as it were, promoting it" (136). "Newtonian vibrations", he says, suggest an analogue for the origin of these "facts"; they do not provide a theory that satisfactorily explains the nervous power to promote visions.

In his "normal" states the claimant "sees" the English scene as if he had seen it before. "There was a vibration from the other world, continued and prolonged into this, the instant that he stept upon that mysterious and haunted ground", as Middleton is made to perceive (*Ancestral Footstep*, 13). Expanding into a narrative the "vibrations" announced in Middleton's walk in the English landscape, both subsequent versions (*Etherege* and *Grimshawe*) record the same subjective impression:

> A bird rose out of the grass, and a little way upward from earth burst into a melody, as if it had broken into a sweet audible flame with which it burst skyward. The lark, the lark! (*Etherege*, 129)
> . . . like one should handle a dream and find it tangible and real, he heard a sound that bewitched him with still another dreamy delight. A bird rose out of the grassy field, and, still soaring aloft, made a cheery melody, rapturous music, as if the whole soul and substance of the winged creature had been distilled into this melody as it vanished skyward.
> "The lark! The lark!", exclaimed the traveller, recognizing the note (*though never heard before) as if his childhood had known it* (*Grimshawe*, 444; emphasis added).

The claimant's preternatural recognition is, in fact, natural. The lark's melody functions as a mediation between a knowledge of nature that distinguishes Old and New World species of birds and a knowledge of nature that "sees" anew apparently forgotten links. "[T]hough never heard before", as Townshend would maintain, or "as if his childhood had known it", as the unwilling-formation-of-memory theorists would speculate, the sound of the lark points to a "remembrance of things past" in a subject who naturally, in his normal state, debunks his own country's amnesia of continuities. His "dreamy delight" may indeed suggest the delights of more modern paramnesias: the effect is of pleasure and contrasts with the conscious fear of the "demon of history" as eternal return.

One of the reasons for Hawthorne's failure to carry through the project of the romances is, according to Nina Baym, the impossibility of accepting the English past as "a valid presence in the American psyche" (Baym, 1976, 254). Still, Hawthorne shows the way to the cure of the same American psyche. If the symptom is collective amnesia, the claimant's represented consciousness can suggest the healing function of paramnesia and its result—seeing the forgotten past not as a stifling burden but as the repressed presence that, by surfacing again, contributes to making the American identity "new" in a context of social functioning secularized both by science and by the ideology of individualism.

The "sins of the fathers"—and the foul corpses that project their decomposing effects on the present of the American Claimant—may be healed in secular anatomies of "psychic states". The Foucauldian notion of social functioning based on the distinction between "healthy" and "unhealthy" bodies (Foucault, 1965) may apply to Hawthorne's attempt at writing the American claim to the past from within, as it may apply to James's own attempt to make true the claim to a sense of the past, by exposing Ralph Pendrel to the effects of "gaining a second consciousness" (James, 1945, 38). As James puts it: "it was blessedly not for the economic question, it was for the historic, the aesthetic, fairly in fact for the cryptic, that he cared" (43). Ralph Pendrel "wanted the unimaginable accidents, the little notes of truth for which the common lenses of history, however the scowling muse might bury her nose, was not sufficiently fine" (49). To achieve something finer than history, James's claimant is willing to become "a ghost of the past"; in this willingness is the beginning of a "cure" that will lend him the right to speak for the future: "And yet I am the future", says a musing Ralph Pendrel in front of his ancestral mansion, "and I dream of making it speak" (47).

Both Hawthorne's American Claimant manuscripts and James's *Sense of the Past* can be read as "allegories" of a national paramnesia. Both explore its functioning, and ultimately become a project for its functionality. The past cannot be excised by any ideological promise of future, but it can be put to use when considered a natural part of each individual psychic self. The morality of Emersonian individualism would be both respected and enhanced by a notion of the past as a subjective process of simultaneous perception of memories and present impulses that lead onward.

Hawthorne did not consistently explore the possibility of such a method of constructing new subjective value for the American individual. Still, given the persistence of focus on the claimant's consciousness, a reading of the manuscripts may legitimately suggest that the claim to an English estate is the occasion to test the practicability of such a method.

Is the claim to an English estate ultimately a claim to the moral "property" of the American individual to become the "heir of all ages"? This Hawthorne himself suggested at the outset of *The Ancestral Footstep*. About a decade later, James's "Passionate Pilgrim" (1871) reformulated virtually the same question: his American heir is "a claimant" who feels "that the land and its culture belong to him" (Edel, 1974, 237), but is his feeling legitimate? In *The Sense of the Past*, almost a belated sequel to the passionate pilgrim's story, the heirship appears legitimate and is founded on the moral value of undergoing a psychically dangerous pursuit of the past, which nonetheless is apparently worth the risk.

Whether the American experience, by historical definition originated within memories of ruptures, may generate new continuities, or whether it generates a new supremacy over the Old World, is not clear. But the fact remains that both Hawthorne and James are constructing the value of the modern subject in the moral prerogative of "possessing" the European scene by seeing it "anew".

"Be assured that the right way can never be that which leads you back to the identical shapes that you long ago left behind": this Alice had already established when reading the effects of Edward Randolph's restored portrait in *The Legends of the Province-House*. The past may return but not in *identical* shapes, and the difference may be constructed into the moral space of progress.

> To articulate the past historically does not mean to recognize it "the way it really was" . . . It means to seize hold of a memory as it flashes up in a moment of danger . . . the danger affects both the content of the tradition, and its receivers (Benjamin, 1969, 255).

This quotation from Benjamin may serve as a comment on both Hawthorne and James or on their common "fine" sensibilities. Their individual predicaments, however, should not be forgotten in repeated crossreadings. James's *Sense of the Past* may function as a twentieth-century point of view from which to read Hawthorne's unfinished romance; but, reversing the focus, Hawthorne's manuscripts are still to be read within a sense of the enormity of evil visible in histories of the past and the present, evil about which James had learned to be "reticent". Murders are not an issue in *The Sense of the Past*; there is guilt, but it is a "sentimental" guilt: the seduction and abandonment of an English cousin hangs over the conscience of the ghosts of the past. For Hawthorne there might be instead a very bloody ancestral footstep, an unredeemed gothic trace, that interferes with the salvific project of the representation of a modern consciousness while "seizing hold of a memory". One may state, as has virtually every interpreter of the unfinished manuscript, that the "danger" of the Civil War reoriented Hawthorne's project and eventually doomed it.

Indeed, in both *Etherege* and *Grimshawe* the "danger" is suggested to be, as it was in *The House of the Seven Gables*, the possible reenactment of a criminal or sorrowful deed from the past. Still the representation of the claimant's consciousness that allows him to see new forms in the old remains at odds with a narration whose plot might be determined by the repetition of a bloody event from the past. Try as he might to superimpose his foot over the imprint on the threshold of the ancestral mansion, the claimant never "takes it in". The footstep does not generate visions or a range of effects to be decoded by the claimant's reflective powers. Hawthorne's design for his projected narration spins around when contemplating the original sign, the ancestral footstep. Neither as the originary cause for the plot nor as the symbol of its effects can the footstep be written in.

The bloody footstep that appealed to Hawthorne's imagination as a trace of the past which would lend meaning to the American's claim stubbornly remains only a gothic sign which, seen from the inside of Hawthorne's laboratory—in his tormented asides—tells the story of the failure of his symbolic method to cope with a perceived "danger". Hawthorne knows that his archaeological finding, the legend told by Mrs. Ainsworth, has to be turned into a symbol related to the original migration. In order to make it the versatile sign of multiple effects, gothic and historical, regressive and progressive, he must determine an original meaning. Is it the sign of a crime in "times of civil dissention", a crime political and religious, the regicide of a fierce Puritan; or is it the sign of a fratricidal family crime that has to do with property and love? Is it stamped by a martyr, as the original legend has it, or by a criminal? Is it the sign of a footstep entering the house or issuing from it? Is it the sign of a son murdering a father, since each son "murders the father at a certain age; or does each father try to accomplish the impossibility of murdering his successor?" (*Etherege*, 327). "But if I could get rid of any great crime on the part of the family it would be better" (*Etherege*, 199), Hawthorne momentarily concludes.

All these hypotheses may be plausible; the projected plots, however, fail to give them "representative form" (219). "The life is not yet breathed into this plot, after all my galvanic efforts" (264): but the footstep as a possible "symbolic exponent" remains, unknown both in origin and effects and yet present as a "bloody" memory, in each version of the American claimant story. The bloody footstep would eventually transmigrate into the *Elixir of Life* manuscripts as the trace of a past of continuity, a bloody track to be found on the leaves of the American wilderness. The relation between the descendant and the bloody trace would never be satisfactorily solved. Neither could it be.

As Charles Swann has noticed, Hawthorne meant to transform the descendant of an English family into the ancestor of himself as an American; the project failed, in Swann's view, because Hawthorne did not find a way to reconcile the wish to be one's own ancestor with the quest for an English descent. Reconciliation, Swann maintains, would prove that "America has been discovered in vain" (Swann, 1991,158). Hawthorne, however, seems to have accounted for the "discovery" of America by his insistence on prototypically American visions of England. The claimant does indeed "discover" the old country, and he does so almost in a repetition of his own English ancestor's "discovery" of America, bringing to the Old World an American foreknowledge that promotes vision. The failure, it seems to me, is not brought about by the fear that America has been discovered in vain, but by Hawthorne's inability to merge the process of "renewing" the past with bloody betrayals.

In the *Legends*, the Young American Woman, Alice, reads Edward Randolph's portrait as the sign of a betrayal that should not be repeated in the future. She tells Hutchinson, the father figure, that he might become a traitor and start a fratricidal war. But the past can be reformed by descendants who see renewed brotherhoods. As a "child of the past" Alice establishes the historical fact that fathers are fratricidal; as an implied reader she suggests the possibility of morally distancing herself from a feud among siblings. In the American Claimant's story the footstep insistently refers to a fratricidal drama; this is not the drama of fathers who kill their sons, or of sons who kill their fathers, but a conflict of equals within a recognized kinship structure. A "fratricide" is staged at the beginning of both *Septimius Felton* and *Septimius Norton*, while in *Grimshawe* the narration begins by setting the story in America immediately after that country's Revolution. In the *Elixir of Life* manuscripts Hawthorne moves the scene to revolutionary America; this does not mean, though, that the connections of the ancestral footstep to an English past are ever denied (on the contrary, Septimius is said to accept his heirship and estate at the end of his mad quest for immortality).

Is the fratricide of the Civil War responsible for the shift? There are biographical reasons to believe so, as most recently Edwin H. Miller has further investigated (Miller, 1991, 461-98). Textual evidence also shows another progression that both renounces the inward method of representation of an Anglo-Saxon memory and removes the footstep from the English scene to the American where its traces connect migration to the Puritan times, to the Indian wars, to the Revolution, and finally to the Civil War. Once moved to the land of the new, bloody fratricidal betrayals may also show traces of betrayals of blood. The newly born fantasy of a national identity of renewed Anglo-Saxon brotherhood may be imperiled not only by the repetition of historical fratricide between kinsmen of the same race, but by the recognition that the new American who calls the killing of an English kinsman "fratricide" can still call the handsome British aristocrat his brother, when he is himself a "miscegenated" being: the half-Puritan and half-Indian Septimius.

FOOTSTEPS OF BLOOD AND *THE ELIXIR OF LIFE*

Upon resuming the ancestral footstep material, probably in 1861 (*Elixir of Life*, 561), Hawthorne does not cast his young American as the heir of all ages returning to his country after his immersion in the English past, but as a conceited young man who attempts to become an immortal hero. Septimius is given a mixed descent, a mad pursuit, and the right age for fighting for his country in its own historical time "of civil dissension", the Revolution. Many are the relations between the American Claimant manuscripts and the two versions of *Septimius Felton* and *Septimius Norton*; the apparent difference is that Hawthorne abandons the pursuit of the past for the pursuit of an endless future. In doing so he replaces the representation of an inward self-construction with the external contemplation of the effects of a mad pursuit undertaken by a deranged but still utopian individual: as Hawthorne reminded himself in *Etherege*, the American ancestor and descendant should be "a man aiming, the wrong way, at some great good for his race" (199).

The phantasmagoria of national memory is seemingly displaced by the investigation of a Faustian theme that, nonetheless, finds its historical origin in the migration of an English aristocrat who carried with him the recipe for the elixir. The renewed quest for the portentous liquid is accelerated by the outbreak of the American Revolution. The connection between theme and time suggests that the pursuit of immortality—eternal youth and the concomitant romantic social utopia—is the legacy of the past to be investigated within a paradigmatic time and place: the Revolution as eternal progress and America as the land of eternally renewed youth.

Alchemy might have seemed to Hawthorne a fruitful compromise between old and new—a form of science left behind by the new science, whose informing principles apply to the new; as Swann has brilliantly shown, relying on Mircea Eliade's *The Forge and the Crucible*, alchemy could stand for revolutionary change and could help in redefining its meaning (Swann, 1991, 240-52). Not differently from the "millenary dream of the alchemist", John Bovee Dods, the most Emersonian of "scientific" mesmerists, wrote in 1850:

> The chariot of science with ever increasing power, magnificence, and glory is destined to pass the boundaries of the mouldering tomb—to snatch immortality from the iron grasps of death, and roll on in living grandeur through the eternal world, gathering new accessions of intellectual beauty and unending delight. Its passengers here are mortal men. There they will be angel, archangel, cherubim, seraphim, and the glorified millions of our race! The mind of man wears the impression of divinity, the stamp of original greatness; and is destined to ripen in mental vigor as the wasteless ages of ETERNITY roll. Hence the very principles of our nature as an impression from the hand of God, forbid us to stand still. Their command is ONWARD (Dods, 1850, 35).

In *Etherege* Hawthorne wrote that "the bitterest satire (if well done) that ever was written" would be the representation of a man provided with a conscience (*Etherege*, 207). With the American Claimant he attempted to give a "consciousness" to such moral conscience. The same satirical impulse may be seen transposed in Septimius's wishful denial of the past or of historical time in his claim to the future. Septimius does not "see" the Revolution while it is happening and does not "remember" either remote or intervening pasts. He does not explore the "reality" that the narrator familiarly describes as the perception of a moment,

> such as I suppose all men feel (at least I can answer for one) where the real scene and picture of life swims, jars, shakes, seems about to be broken up and dispersed, like the picture in a smooth pond, when we disturb its smooth mirror by throwing a stone . . . (*Septimius Felton*, 101).

For Septimius the quest for reality is tuned into the unreality of the pursuit. He believes he can "live" outside the "boundaries of the mouldering tomb" in a perpetual onward. Scientific progress and transcendental "onwards", emphatically claimed by the Emersonian Dods, are for Septimius the utopian project to be worked into the reality of his country. His utopia sounds like the *compte-rendu* of Hawthorne's own philosophical age—almost a satire of Emerson's "Fate" in *The Conduct of Life* (1860)—under the aegis of a monomania that links scientific progress to the "alchemic cure" of social and historical evils: through alchemy history can become the healing utopia of the known. Once his eternal youth has been achieved, Septimius says, "having seen so much of affairs, and having lived so many hundred years, I will sit down and write a history, such as histories ought to be and never have been" (*Septimius Felton*, 173). Septimius's statement comes after the fancied accomplishment of a social cure—the "devising and putting in execution [of] the remedies for [mankind's] chills" (171)—that would debunk all the "fragments" of contemporary "science", physical, philosophical, and political. In Septimius's new world there will be democracy and no war, social equality for women and the enjoyment of pleasure, all the more intense because the experience of evil is to be part of his omnivorous life.

In Septimius's utopia there is no mention of hybridism. He pretends to be the collective "we", the same republican "we" that the revolutionary setting of his adventurous pursuit shows in the process of becoming historical reality. Still he is a hybrid and surrounded by hybrids. Hybridism is everywhere—in the forms of a Goethean natural world of plants and of an American natural world of humans. Septimius himself is a "miscegenated" American, and a student of plant hybridism.

In the American Claimant manuscripts there are allusions to hybridized spiders and gardens, and to hybridized cultures. Hybridized spiders are the result of the old doctor's scientific experiments; he hopes they might secrete some mysterious panacea, but they produce only gigantic cobwebs. Hybridized cultures and human hybrids are linked to women's bodies: Alice hums "negro melodies" in *The Ancestral Footstep*; in *Etherege*, Elsie's Indian craft, her beadwork, should "intimate an origin not exactly normal, but yet nothing extravagant or unwomanly" (333). In *Grimshawe*, Crusty Hannah teaches beadwork to little Elsie, "the kind of embroidery . . . she learnt from Crusty Hannah . . . was emblematic perhaps, of that creature's strange mixture of races". The little girl's own artifacts are refined versions of wild savage fantasies that she divines in her teacher's primitive craft. Crusty Hannah's own nature is defined as terribly wild and unnatural. A notation introduces her— "<Crusty Hannah is a mixture of Indian and Negro, & as some say, Monkey"> (344)—and is frequently recalled in the narrative (346; 409; 425). Crusty Hannah's "monstrosity" comes to the foreground as the trait of Kezia, Septimius's aunt. Kezia's ancestry, however, unlike Crusty Hannah's, and like Septimius's, is Indian and Anglo-Saxon, and not black. The common ancestry of these three hybrids is not white or black but Indian. Kezia's upsettingly "wild" nature matches Septimius's own. It is a nature that has dreadful effects: the Indian blood may be responsible for the hero's unquenchable passions, but at the same time his unquenchable passions are an American reality when he kills the fair youth from England. This may be the deeper "monstrousness that had grown out of his hybrid race" (*Septimius Felton*, 40). The "natural force of blood" binds kin together (*Grimshawe*, 377); when the force of blood is "unnatural" it begets monsters. In *Etherege*, the characteristic trait of evil attributed to the English cousin is derived from his Italian blood, as often happened in classic gothic tales. Thence came the evil "in his nature, coming from the past, in his blood" (*Etherege*, 268). This gothic character was not convincing enough: Italian poison "won't do", Hawthorne comments (269). American gothic could substitute "swarthy Indians" for "swarthy Italians". Still, Septimius is both the descendant of a literary code and the embodiment of a utopia perceived as the all-white American dream of the Revolution: he is an American who goes to college, is trained to become a minister, and strives to make both the Puritan and Indian legacies his own.

There is one detail in one of the claimant's feverish states that appears incongruous and that may be seen as leading to the transformation from European to American hybridism. On examining the wound inflicted by the English relative's gun on the young man's body, the surgeon wonders about the mark of a previous bullet wound. Even if not directly questioned and apparently unconscious, Etherege answers him:

> <There should be a light wildness in the patient's remark to the surgeon, which he cannot prevent, though he is conscious of it.> "It was an Indian bullet," said the patient, still fancying himself gone astray in the past, "shot at me in battle, two or three hundred years hereafter."
>
> "Ah; he has served in the East Indies," said the surgeon . . . The patient did not care to take the trouble which would have been involved in correcting the surgeon's surmise . . . (*Grimshawe*, 453).

The Indian bullet goes back to a time when Indians had no bullets and the English colonies were in their formation: though conscious of it, the patient unconsciously utters the remark and consciously does not bother to correct the surgeon's surmise. It is indeed hard to imagine what the correction could have been. True to facts or true to a psychic law that connects seemingly unconnected and unreasonably distant events? The psychic law is apparently stronger than the good doctor's healing remark. The surgeon's remark links the claimant's Indian memory to another land which had recently been bloodied by slaughter. The surgeon's East Indies would remind the prospective 1860s reader of a recent patriotically hailed event, the suppression of the Indian Mutiny of 1857. Thanks to the gallantry of outnumbered British soldiers the British native armies, turned rebellious, were defeated. As a consequence of their bloody betrayal, on August 2, 1858, the East India Company, which since 1600 had ruled over India, handed over the Government to the Crown.

The claimant's paramnesia allows for a possible interpretation of the Indian wars as both a betrayal of national symbolism—natives of India and Britain being under the same flag—and a necessity of reestablishing blood differences within the progressive course of the Empire. The claimant's body, though finally cured by English healing men, still supposedly wears the scar of the Indian bullet, side by side with the scar of the bullet of his English cousin.

The Indian and the English pasts of the young American may both be seen as murderous betrayals and progressive necessities; by turning Septimius into a hybrid of English and Indian ancestry Hawthorne makes murderous betrayals not betrayals of the flag but betrayals of blood. Septimius is twice "murderer" and "traitor": he kills his English relative, and he kills his aunt. In both cases there is a justification: in the first it is a historical event (the Revolution), in the second a scientific pursuit (to test a new recipe for the elixir). Though Septimius never "sees" the blood traces his English ancestor left on the leaves of the American wilderness, he acts in his footstep, a thing that the American Claimant is never made to do. The bloody trace of the progenitor appears to have been left by a man who emigrated to America after a murderous event; the same man carried with him two things, the secret of immortality and a miscegenated future. The American ancestor as immigrant is bound to become a cultural hybrid in the American wilderness: he is the "Indianized" white chief of the tribe.

From the ancestor's cultural mixing issues a "natural", yet "unnatural", race of hybrids. The "white" cultural hermaphrodite, the

Natty Bumppo of Cooper's foundational national myth of universal brotherhood between the same Father's children, becomes the ancestor of children with "unnatural" blood and too many pasts to be reckoned with.

Too many pasts: once continuity with Anglo-Saxon ancestry becomes a cultural necessity, as it did in the late 1850s, a renewed vision may account for an American claim to the past. Plants and humans can be transplanted in a project of mutual satisfaction: the New England population may be transplanted in Britain and vice versa (*Etherege*, 246). As a consequence the American's own continuity in the New World becomes an issue: "Posterity! An American can have none" is the comment on Etherege's "anticipations" of a future "built" for his descendants.

The same denial of an American posterity in the search for eternal youth is represented in the tension between too many pasts—British, Puritan, Indian. At the center of this tension is Septimius himself, the all-American, miscegenated, "unnatural" descendant who claims to be an eternal ancestor.

The "natural force of blood" can convey both a gothic and a utopian sense of history: killing the British brother, or the miscegenated American aunt, does not erase the fact that Septimius, on a quest for eternal youth, is the paradigm of hopes and fears, cast as both the descendant of the migrant and the prospective ancestor of an American breed, whose story happens to be written when the Civil War presumably required new introspective investigations of the American experience.

In the representation of the Revolution in *Septimius Felton* and *Septimius Norton* the narrator invokes the similarity between the Revolution and the Civil War, both the effects of a "plague" or of the opening of the "old pit" of the past. "Out of that old grave had come a new plague, that slew the far-off progeny of those who had first died by it" (*The Ancestral Footstep*, 9). "We stand afar off, but still may know sorrow best, from the experiences of our own day, of what emotions were in the atmosphere of that April morning, nearly ninety years ago . . . we know something of that time now . . . we that have seen . . . watched" (*Septimius Norton*, 216; 217). The effects of the past(s) are now the collective experience of a historical present and bring back both the desire for a utopian future and the "horror" of deep-seated fears when confronted with the reality of the resistance of the American past to becoming "usable" for new secessions or renewed unions.

In the piece "Chiefly About War Matters" (1862) and in *Our Old Home* (1863) Hawthorne sees his own fictions of the past becoming "true" in history; in the process, his dream of a "neutral ground" where opposite effects can coexist is shattered:

> There is no remoteness of life and thought, no hermetically sealed seclusion, except possibly, that of the grave, into which the disturbing influences of this war do not penetrate. Of course, the general heart-quake of the country long ago knocked at my cottage door, and compelled me, reluctantly, to suspend the contemplation of certain fantasies, to which, according to my harmless custom, I was endeavoring to give a sufficient lifelike aspect to admit of their figuring in a romance ("Chiefly About War Matters", 1883, 299).
>
> The Present, the Immediate, the Actual, has proved too potent for me. It takes away not only my scanty faculty, but even my desire for imaginative composition, and leaves me sadly content to scatter a thousand peaceful fantasies upon the hurricane that is sweeping us all along with it, possibly, into a Limbo where our nation and its polity may be as literally the fragments of a shattered dream as my unwritten Romance" (*Our Old Home*, 1970, 4).

There is no doubt that Hawthorne is writing, as Charles Swann has remarked, an "obituary to the American Claimant materials" (Swann, 1991, 180). Hawthorne's obituary shows the lucid recognition of the creed of a lifetime. The prospective ruin of this creed and of its artistic forms emanates not from the English past, but from the American present: "But the ruin of my own country is perhaps all that I am destined to witness; and that immense catastrophe (though I am strong in the faith that there is a national lifetime for a thousand years in us yet) would serve any man well enough as his final spectacle on earth" (*Our Old Home*, 1970, 88).

This is a final spectacle that, for the last time, to my knowledge, revives the metaphor of phantasmagoria that Hawthorne repeatedly evoked in *Etherege* and *Grimshawe*. In "Chiefly About War Matters" the metaphor is applied to the direct observation of the Civil War, both a reality and a deceit. Describing the march toward Manassas of the Northern armies, pursuing an enemy turned invisible by strategic withdrawal, Hawthorne portrays the Union soldiers as seeing only "ghosts" in the shape of "Quaker guns", planted by the enemy to simulate a presence: "almost with their first step into the Virginia mud, the phantasmagory of a countless host and impregnable ramparts, before which they had so long been quiescent, dissolved quite away". Such "overwhelming effect" played by the Rebels is "ludicrous" but for the Union soldiers it is "historically" functional, because it both exposes the war as a deceit and assesses its reality.

As a reader of Hawthorne's real dreams, in which palimpsestic memories keep surfacing, I conclude with a palimpsestic popular writing of the modern era:

> Their blood has wash'd out their foul footsteps' pollution,
> no refuge could save the hireling and slave from the terror of flight
> or the gloom of the grave . . .

These anti-British and anti-loyalist lines from the revolutionary patriotic song "The Star-Spangled Banner", written in 1814 by Francis Scott Key, were increasingly omitted from official printings after the 1850s (Sonneck, 1914). The omission was necessary in the construction of Anglo-Saxonism, the invention of a common blood that would unify the splendid British past and present with the American future (Hitchens, 1990, 11). Still one may legitimately ask: while the Civil War was raging, "whose" blood was to wash out the "foul footsteps' pollution" when the "pollution" was in the "old" American blood itself? "Stained scenes and events" from the past find continuity in the new forms of the present, but, Hawthorne acknowledged, these scenes and events may be too potent, and the bloody footstep appears unlikely to be washed away from the American wilderness.

MELVILLE

VIEW OF COPPS HILL, BOSTON.

Part One

Herman Melville and the Past
as an American Sourcebook

From the dire caverns made by ghostly miners,
let the explosion, dreadful as volcanoes,
Heave the broad town, with all its wealth and people,
    Quick to destruction!
Still shall the banner of the King of Heaven
Never advance where I'm afraid to follow:
While that precedes me with an open bosom,
    War, I defy thee.

> —Nathaniel Niles, "Bunker Hill, or the American Hero"

Books are the best type of the influence of the past, and perhaps we shall get at the truth,—learn the amount of this influence more conveniently,—by considering their value alone.

> —Ralph Waldo Emerson, "The American Scholar"

Wo unto you, when all
men shall speak well of you!
for so did their fathers to
the false prophets.

> —Luke vi; 26
> (underlined by Herman Melville, after 1846)

AN AUTHENTIC BOOK OF THE PAST:
ISRAEL POTTER, REVOLUTIONARY SOLDIER

In July 1854, Herman Melville started serializing in *Putnam's Monthly* his eighth book, *Israel Potter: His Fifty Years of Exile*. His most recent novel, *Pierre* (1852), had been severely attacked by reviewers, mainly on grounds of indecency. *Israel Potter*, Melville reassured his publisher, would be different: it was to be a tale that would "contain nothing of any sort to shock the fastidious", and "with very little reflective writing in it" (Bezanson, 1982, 182). The first installment of *Israel Potter* appeared with the subtitle, "A Fourth-of-July Story"; this was perhaps an editorial choice of *Putnam's*, as part of a current display of patriotic feeling, shared also by the more established *Democratic Review*, which had published Hawthorne's *Legends of the Province-House* (Dekker, 1987, 190). Melville's readers were thus led to expect a narrative of the country's illustrious recent past, its Revolution, within the renewed fervor for national definition.

Israel Potter relates the story of a Revolutionary soldier, one of those homespun minutemen who have become the pride of the American tradition. It is nonetheless a sad story: Israel, a young man from the Berkshires, fights at Bunker Hill, is taken prisoner by the British, ends up in England, escapes, becomes a spy and serves Benjamin Franklin in Paris, then sails forth with John Paul Jones, is his companion in Whitehaven, survives the epic battle between the *Bon Homme Richard* and the *Serapis*, is again taken prisoner by the English, and witnesses Ethan Allen's arrival in chains in Britain. Once again a fugitive, as an American soldier in the enemy's land, he finally settles down in London, where he lives for 45 years, supporting himself and his English wife and children (all but one die) with the scanty means provided by his work as a chair-mender. In 1826 the American Consul offers him a passage home. He eventually goes back to his country hoping to be granted a pension on account of his war services, but he dies with his hopes unfulfilled.

For his new novel Melville had set aside, probably in the 1840s, a little pamphlet, *Life and Remarkable Adventures of Israel R. Potter*

(1824), which he had in mind in 1849 in London since he recorded in his *Journal* that he had bought an eighteenth-century map of the city to "serve up the Revolutionary narrative of the beggar" (Melville, 1948, 75). He also apparently used several other lesser sources on the Revolutionary era—most notably Roberts C. Sands, *Life and Correspondence of John Paul Jones* (1830), James F. Cooper, *History of the Navy of the United States* (rev. ed. 1840), and Ethan Allen's own *A Narrative of Colonel Ethan Allen's Captivity* (1779). The number and identification of Melville's historical sources is still a matter of debate (Bezanson, 1982; Cohen, 1991). What is certain is Melville's statement in the preface to *Israel Potter* that his novel preserved "almost as in a reprint, Israel Potter's autobiographical story".

The author of the supposed autobiography of Israel Potter, a native of Cranston, Rhode Island, was Henry Trumbull, publisher, writer, and editor, who guarantees the authenticity of character and facts in his booklet by appending a letter by a former Revolutionary soldier who had met Israel Potter during the war. The autobiography could then be presented as an authentic document of Revolutionary times, and as such could be considered a respectable historical source for a novel (Bezanson, 1982, 184-7).

As a literary rewrite of an authentic document, Melville's novel invites critics to revive classic questions on the nature of historical novels, such as: what is their relation to the source or sources? What is the relation between a primary source and the others that are referred to in the novel? What is it that makes a source historical? Are there grounds for similarity (or difference) between historical writing and fictional writing? What value is to be attached to historical truth or to fictional truth? This novel also invites an exploration of the controversial, contemporary question of whether culture is part of history or not. If it is, "authenticity" gives way to the verisimilitude of parallel versions of historical discourses, and Melville's exhibited historical "fidelity" should be seen as the poetic variant of historical narrations.

The "fastidious" may be alerted now, as they were quickly alerted at the first appearance of *Israel Potter*, although on different grounds than those which had made *Pierre* scandalous. Soon after the novel had run its course in *Putnam's*, one of its editors strongly attacked it for its lack of historical fidelity to the source:

> Mr Melville departs considerably from his original. He makes Israel born in Berkshire, Mass., and brings him acquainted with Paul Jones, as he was not. How far he is justified in the historical liberties he has taken, would be a curious case of literary casuistry (*Putnam's*, V, 1855, 545).

This line of reasoning has continued into the present. The authors of a 1984 *William and Mary Quarterly* article complain that Melville's novel "blurred the fine distinction between history and literature" (Chako, Kulchsar, 1984, 366); they eventually disclaim the historical reliability of Trumbull's account and even the truthfulness of what was supposedly told him by Israel Potter himself. Other critics of Melville make similar attacks when, wondering about the place *Israel Potter* should take in the writer's canon, they argue that its major fault is lack of unity—a unity which could be provided either by a stricter fidelity to the autobiographical account, or by a larger play of literary invention. As Newton Arvin put it, Melville wavers,

> . . . between faithfulness and freedom, following the original narrative up to a certain point, then taking off for a series of episodes mostly of his own invention, and finally, in the last five chapters, returning warily to his source and bringing the book to a hurried and perfunctory close (Arvin, 1950, 245).

What still makes Melville's novel a "curious case of literary casuistry" is the discrepancy that it presents between a faithful rewriting of a source, reliable or unreliable as it might be, yet considered in itself a historical document, and a rewriting that relies primarily on literary invention. As a result, by lingering mainly on the opposition between the Aristotelian category of *inventio* and the "facts" of the autobiography as historical document, the role both of *dispositio* and *elocutio* in literary and historical writings has been overlooked, while both Trumbull's *Life* and Melville's novel provide an interesting ground of analysis precisely in the comparison of the different strategies through which both texts aim at suggesting the "authentic" discourse of the American past.

In *Israel Potter*, chapters two through six closely follow the autobiography but in a narration strongly reminiscent of eighteenth-century fictions (a contemporary reviewer noticed, to his satisfaction, that now Melville seemed to write like Defoe); the remaining twenty, while essentially respecting the sequence of the autobiography, introduce new episodes and new characters, both "invented" and historical. Melville's characteristic, symbolic texture is announced in the first major departure from the source, the novel's incipit (ch. 1), thus marking both the linguistic shift, and the departure from the source's factual arrangement. Starting with Israel's encounter with Benjamin Franklin (ch. 7), the events of Potter's life are increasingly ordered by a symbolic logic that revolves around the paradigms of escape and revolutionary action, versus imprisonment and delayed release. The closing chapter (26) symmetrically frames the narration with Israel coming back to the home of its beginning.

A pluralism of narrative modes integrates the "mimicry" of Trumbull's "plain-style". The comic mode of a picaresque narration is amalgamated with satire (its high point in the Franklin chapters); with the epic (the battle of the *Serapis*); with the gothic (Israel entombed alive and in the brick furnace); with tragic pathos (the Dickensian narrative of Israel's life among the lowly); and finally by the elegy of the octogenarian's homecoming.

Many literary influences have been detected in *Israel Potter*, from Edgar Allan Poe and Washington Irving, to Dante, Bunyan and others (Cohen, 1986). This is not surprising, as Melville's texts are conspicuously characterized by both polyphony and intertextuality. Melville was a voracious and idiosyncratic reader, as is proved by the evidence of several biographical documents and by the extensive annotations to be found in the books still extant that he borrowed or owned. A literary evidence of Melville's own method of reading could be seen in *Pierre*, in the hero's infatuation with Plinlimmon's "Chronometricals and Horologicals", a text, like Trumbull's *Life*, "tattered" and printed on "sleazy paper". Men such as Pierre, we are told,

> fasten with unaccountable fondness upon the merest rag of old printed paper—some shred of a long-exploded advertisement perhaps—and read it, and study it, and re-read it, and pore over it, and fairly agonize themselves over this miserable, sleazy paper rag . . . (Melville, 1984, 243).

Everything, from "advertisements" and newspaper clippings to *Don Quijote*, and the Bible, etc., Melville read cannibalistically; and he constantly incorporated, transformed, and commented upon such "sources", thus making them the texture of his fiction.

The opposition between fact and imagination, his fidelity or infidelity to a source, is not an issue when "literary" sources are considered, but seems to be held as crucial when focusing on the relation between a literary text and its historical sources, thus proving that literary discourse is more easily assimilated into "culture" than historical discourse. On the other hand, our contemporary reliance on literary evidence in historical discourse can be seen as the conscious application of a cultural practice initiated by historical novels. As Eric Hobsbawm convincingly argues, "inventions" have become part of history (Hobsbawm, 1983). Melville's *Israel Potter* can be added to the list of such "artifacts", since it has been used as a data source on the life of the real soldier in *The Appleton Encyclopedia of American Biography* (1888) and in Charles Edward Potter's *Genealogies of the Potter Families and Their Descendants* (1888) (Madison, 1982, 280). Melville's one chapter and a half dedicated to Ethan Allen, though derived from Allen's own autobiography, was in its turn the preferred historical account of the *Western Literary Messenger*, where it was published under the title "Ethan Allen's Captivity" in September, 1855. The *Messenger's* editors reshuffled Melville's work (published in book-form a few months before) and, with a rare, historically humorous twist, turned Israel Potter into an "exiled Englishman" who, "strolling around Pendennis Castle", chanced to hear one of the American hero's "outbursts of indignation and madness" (*Western Literary Messenger*, xxv, 1, 1855, 21). Israel Potter's story then could be turned into history, because paradoxically its "literary" rendition was perceived as culturally more "true".

Israel Potter—His Fifty Years of Exile remains a particularly intriguing case study for inquiries into the relationships or the resonances that "texts" of a similar or different "nature" establish with each other and with their cultural or historical contexts. At the same time Melville's method of writing invites an intertextual reading that aims not so much at assessing the issue of "authenticity" of facts or the definite identification of sources and their (infinite) numbers, but at an interpretation of some resonances and transformations. Sources can be traditionally considered within a genetically-oriented type of investigation: as such, Trumbull's *Life* is inscribed in Melville's text. Or they can be seen as discourses that parallel the text under consideration within a shared cultural process of producing meaning. Both perspectives are helpful in the investigation of Melville's *Israel Potter*, a text which claims as its poetic principle the transformation of a historical document into a literary work. As a literary work within the genre of historical novels its specificity demands an analytical description of the narrative strategies through which "sources" become tropes of discourse and eventually change the literary way to tell history within the tradition initiated by the *Waverley Novels*.

Whereas in the same tradition, Hawthorne chooses to half-bury his half-effaced palimpsestic writings, Melville exposes his sources by turning them into textual figures of a process of interpretation. It was perhaps both the awareness of the virtually endless multiplicity of "sources" and the insistent deferral of the certainty of meaning that made Melville display and pile up his sources, as *Moby Dick*'s cetology makes apparent. In the perspective of narrations that move from the past to the present, sources become the "outlandish old guide-books" that shape the expectations of Young Americans such as Redburn—who proudly records that his grandfather had fought at Bunker Hill. The age's concern with a "usable past" is fictionalized through the poetic reworking of a book of the past: for Melville, as Agostino Lombardo suggests, the relation to the past is a relation to its books

(Lombardo, 1961, 185). This dialogic relation may orient the reader's perception of their "usability" for the future.

Whereas Hawthorne sees phantasmagoric shows as a metaphor suggesting the muted laws governing the world and its past, Melville relies on the metaphor of the "library" to penetrate the "world of appearances": for him the act of "reading" is equivalent to the act of "seeing". A phantasmagoria appears in *Pierre* as the sign of the protagonist's inability to "read". His eyes "blinked and shut", in a "foretaste of death", his pupils repeatedly rolling "away from him", Pierre sees "the phantasmagoria of the Mount of the Titans". This dream turns the image of Enceladus into his own face wearing a look of "prophetic discomfiture and woe" (Melville, 1984, 2, 402). And where Pierre's "random knowledge of ancient fables" fails to elucidate the phantasmagoric meaning, the narrator himself aptly provides bookish clues both to the Berkshires landscape and to the incestuous myth of Enceladus' birth and doom.

The project of romantic totality of vision is mocked in "Benito Cereno", the most "phantasmagoric" of Melville's tales of the past. In the tricks of light on the ship's stage, Amasa Delano's imperfect sight leads to a faulty perception of the show put up for him; at the same time the "reading" of the source which follows serves as the inverted lens through which the representation of the past is to be measured anew.

In contrast to "Benito Cereno", *Israel Potter* claims its "authenticity" not by quoting a historical document, but by showing the process through which a source is "read" and turned into a fiction of the past. Melville's 1854 novel is the most self-reflexive example of his method of historical writing (Henderson, 1974, 140): as such it shows an experimental quality which is different from, and yet compatible with, Hawthorne's own tales of the past. Sharing the contemporary imperative to write the past anew, both Hawthorne and Melville have forged narrative codes for the the representation of the past which appear familiar to the late twentieth-century reader. In mainstream American literature, Hawthorne's "historic consciousness" may connect to the fictional methods of Henry James and William Faulkner, while Melville's self-reflexive use of the books of the past reminds us of those "historical fictions" that Christine Brooke-Rose has called "palimpsest histories", such as John Barth's *The Sotweed Factor* (1960), and Robert Coover's *The Public Burning* (1977) (Brooke-Rose, 1991, 181-90).

THE *LIFE AND REMARKABLE ADVENTURES* OF *ISRAEL POTTER*: THE SOURCE

The *Life and Remarkable Adventures of Israel Potter*, Melville's primary historical "source", is presented by its author, Henry Trumbull, as the authentic record of the life of a Revolutionary soldier. Its form is that of a vindication of the "aged veteran"'s claim to a pension as a reward for his services to the country. It is a humble-toned vindication, addressed to true American spirits, implicitly able to realize Israel Potter's right to share with them "the blessings produced by American valour". Its rhetoric supports the necessity of an atonement for what is presented as either a momentary injustice in the national system, or an exceptional persecution by Fate. Israel Potter's real story is all the more exceptional because it seems contrary to the laws of justice and progress affirmed by the American Revolution.

Trumbull's text—an excellent demonstration of Hayden White's theory of the import of rhetoric in historical documents—tells its story evoking notions of patriotism and American exceptionalism that reflect the celebratory national mood of the 1820s.

The decade of the 1820s was crucial to the shaping of a national rhetoric that celebrated the Revolution as both the Puritan forefathers' realized legacy and a new start in history (Bercovitch, 1976). Historical self-knowledge was very much in demand, and several historical societies were established in the years between 1820 and 1828 (Kammen, 1978, 26). In 1824, the year of Trumbull's publication, patriotic Boston citizens began raising funds for the erection of the Bunker Hill Monument. The actual construction started just one year later with a grand ceremony and an inaugural speech by Daniel Webster. Welcoming the erection of the monument and celebrating the forty aged veterans in the audience, Webster voiced the current interpretation of the American Revolution as "a prodigy of modern times", an extraordinary event in the history of human progress. The Americans, who had proved their extraordinary character both in war and in the years that followed it, may well take up their burden and their reward. As Webster says:

> And now let us indulge an honest exultation in the conviction of the benefit which the example of our country has produced, and is likely to produce, on human freedom and human happiness. Let us endeavor to comprehend, in all its magnitude, and to feel in all its importance, the part assigned to us in the great drama of human affairs . . . The principle of free governments adheres to the American soil. It is bedded in it, immovable as its mountains (Webster, 1895, 19; 24-5).

After the South American revolutionary crisis, American exceptionalism and the natural and geographical foundation of the democratic ideal found their authoritative validation in the Monroe declaration of 1823. By claiming American independence on a world scale, the political discourse that led to the Monroe doctrine gave a new twist to the much talked-about opposition between the Old World and the New, and the difference was more and more stressed on behalf of the new country. Furthermore, after the 1812 war with England, more than 200 autobiographical accounts of patriotic Revolutionary soldiers were published (Dorson, 1953).

Potter's autobiography is written as an understatement of Revolutionary celebration and an overstatement of American/British difference. Israel Potter, American born, spirited patriot and heroic soldier, proudly believes in those principles of origin, exceptionalism, self-realization, and progress that support the image of post-revolutionary America. The contradiction between this figure of a model citizen and the other figure of the victim of his own Americanism is solved in the contrastive representation of his miserable life in Britain—a place of poverty and social injustice—and his past idyllic life in the new country: hence his dream of present-day America as the haven of hope and justice is unshakeable.

As Trumbull's Israel Potter puts it:

Let those of my countrymen who thus imagine themselves miserable amid plenty, cross the Atlantic and visit the miserable habitations of real and unaffected woe—if their hearts are not destitute of feeling, they will return satisfied to their own peaceful and happy shores, and pour forth the ejaculations of gratitude to that universal parent, who has given them abundance and exempted them from the thousand ills, under the pressure of which a great portion of his children drag the load of life . . . Britain, imperious Britain, who once boasted the freedom of her government and the invincible power of her arms—now finds herself reduced to the humiliating necessity of receiving lessons from those whom till late she dispised [sic] as slaves!—while our own country on the other hand, like a phenix [sic] from her ashes, having emerged from a long, expensive and bloody war, and established a constitution upon the broad and immovable basis of national equality, now promises to become the permanent residence of peace, liberty, science, and national felicity—But, to return to the tale of my own sufferings . . . (Trumbull, 1982, 76-7).

Once the difference between the Old and the New World has been established, Israel's personal experience becomes a generalizable experience and works as an admonition for his own American countrymen, since it suggests the paradox of the morally unacceptable analogy between themselves and the English.

Throughout the autobiography Israel's voice fulfills the Aristotelian requirements of the good speaker's character: he constantly shows Good Principle, Good Sense, Good Will and a more than friendly disposition towards his audience. His case is strengthened by his own meek but firm faithfulness to such traits which he makes clear are the birthright of any "true blooded Yankee". In addition, historically representative men like Benjamin Franklin and General Putnam, as well as the British King and the English friends of America, Horne Tooke and James Bridges, all recognize Israel's good character and associate it with his native nation. Israel's traits are shown at work in the deeds of his life: as a young man he leaves his family home to go west, acting, in the true pioneer spirit, as a model for the 1820s (the years of the rise of the new West); he goes to fight at Bunker Hill, but only after having finished plowing his field (as General Putnam, whom the national rhetoric celebrated as the American Cincinnatus, is said to have done); in the Revolutionary War he conducts himself as a valorous and modest soldier (modesty was one of the main character traits attributed to Washington); in England he keeps his Franklinian or Yankee enterprising spirit almost intact, adapting himself to any humble job he can find, until he is defeated by that country's brutality.

The final proof of the Old World's indignities comes when Israel is forced to become a beggar, in the time of peace following the end of the Napoleonic Wars. "Begging" becomes the means through which Trumbull is able to differentiate Israel's petition for a just reward from the degrading condition he suffered abroad. The begging motif is linked with the motif of imposture, when Israel tells of those London beggars "that possess the faculty of assuming any character that may best suit their purpose" (62). These con-men are liable to take up the mask of a discharged soldier and unrecognized patriot, showing off a fake "honorable scar of a wound, received in Egypt, or at Waterloo, at Trafalgar" (63). Their act is successful, while Israel, the true war victim, is denied alms because he is American born. In an ironic reversal, his begging is treated like "a vile imposture", undertaken in order to obtain in England "the support" his own country had denied him. In the rhetoric of the vindication, this charge against Israel aims at arousing the reader's moral indignation. The community of readers should prove the falsity of the English accusation against their country by rewarding, not with alms but with a hero's salary, the unfortunate patriot, a truly loyal American.

Trumbull makes Israel Potter, both as voice and character, prove insistently that he is "true", because truthful, thus honoring his American "birthright" even in extremity. To make his vindication successful Trumbull relies on the premise that the character's historical truth is what is perceived as such by his readers, e.g. his native American qualities, defined in opposition to the Old World.

That readers could perceive the *Life and Remarkable Adventures of Israel Potter* as true to history is shown also in a quite recent instance. Richard Dorson comments on the *Life*:

Compare H. Melville's fine tale of Israel Potter with the humble account it rewrites, and notice how closely the artist follows the veteran's story life. Melville recognized an honest, dramatic, and peculiarly American record in the odd little book hawked through the country by Yankee peddlers (Dorson, 1953, 14).

For Dorson—who is famous for his distinction between folklore and fakelore—the autobiography is an authentic document, useful in reconstructing the nation's history; convinced of its historical value, Dorson acts as an interpreter of Melville's own "recognition" as a reader. To Dorson the historical value of the *Life* is found in its qualifications, in its being an "honest" and "peculiarly American" record: these are the qualities overstressed for a rhetorical purpose, the vindication, in Trumbull's text. One could say that what ultimately makes a true historical source of the *Life and Remarkable Adventures of Israel Potter* are not so much the events recorded in it, but the rhetoric of its discourse, based as it is on a resistent historical and cultural pact concerning the interpretation of American history.

Israel Potter, His Fifty Years of Exile: A Parallel, a Type, and a Prophecy

Israel Potter does not speak in tones of vindication, but in those of Americanism as dramatic tension. The novel has been read as the parable of an everyman overcome by history (Keyssar, 1969), or in more recent historicist interpretations, as the story of the defeat of Americanism emerging from the debate on the Revolution (Gilmore, 1977; Karcher, 1980; Rogin, 1983; McWilliams, 1984; Zaller, 1986). Melville's "revolutionary narrative" can also be read within the tension originated by "reading" a truthful "text" of American history and challenging its rhetoric in the name of the same native values it means to vindicate. As John Samson has recently argued, in Melville's work sources should be seen as "a Bakhtinian 'dialogism' of discourses" which reveal his own "thematic and stylistic intentions" (Samson, 1989, 12). More radically, the source's rhetoric may become a theme of his narration: the rhetoric of vindication of the source, which posits that there might be no incongruity between the celebration of the American experience and its actual outcome in the individual destiny of Israel Potter, is re-written in Melville's text as the rhetoric of the motif of exile, in which is exposed the supposed reconcilability between the American self and his nation, or between ideal America and its historical realization.

Melville's text is a historical novel which transforms an "authentic" historical document into a poetic discourse of history. Paul Ricoeur has pointed out that in any "chronicle" there is a first symbolization of temporality that might be turned by the historical interpreter into "the experience of historicality". "Every narration" says Ricoeur, "combines two dimensions in various proportions, one chronological, the other nonchronological . . . the configurational dimension, according to which the plot construes significant wholes out of scattered events" (Ricoeur, 1984, 178-9). Whereas the "significant wholes" in Trumbull's narrative show the value of progression in contrast to the real "events" of Israel Potter's life, Melville's novel constructs its "significant wholes" by reshuffling the plot construction. *Israel Potter*'s narration is characterized both by contraction and prolonged stasis of action, and by the insistent "configuration" of three tropes—type, parallel and prophecy—each related to the process of interpretation of Melville's source in significant variants, reflected in characterization, time and space expansions, narrator-reader functions, and plot causality.

Since the three tropes intersect with each other in two often discussed "departures" from the source—a description of the Berkshire landscape, and the Franklin episode—a detailed analysis of them may serve as a description of Melville's rewriting method of historical narration.

In the long opening description of the Berkshire landscape, Israel as a type is structured as a parallel to American nature and history, and his story is prefigured within a "prophetical" anticipation. Moreover, the relation between the narrator and the implied reader suggests the recognition of both type and parallel in the present of the described landscape. The first chapter, entitled "The Birthplace of

Israel", romantically begins with, "The traveller . . . will find ample food for poetic reflection". This traveller, styled as one with a preference for travelling by horse, an eccentric by contemporary standards in means of locomotion, becomes the invoked "you" of the ideal reader. The narratorial eye yields to a communal "you behold", establishing both identity and distance, thus setting up a parallel vision.

The Berkshires were the culturally invented American equivalent of the English Lake Region. Hawthorne and Melville, but also Oliver Wendell Holmes, lived there at the same time. Thoreau, who visited in 1844, recorded his impressions in *A Week on the Concord and Merrimack Rivers* (1849) as those of a traveller walking on what seemed "a road for the pilgrim to enter upon who would climb to the gates of heaven" or to the glorious wonder of American nature, Mount Greylock, from whose summit the surrounding "gorgeous tapestry" strongly contrasts with "the forlorn world" of civilization below (Thoreau, 1985, 147). Melville's eccentric traveller, not differently from Thoreau's, is offered a vision of natural grandeur. The semantics of Melville's vision, however, more ostensibly dwell on the continuity between the past and the present both as natural to the soil and as resistant and ruined artifacts, products of "ancient industry". The still standing "framework of ancient buildings" and the walls built by the early settlers—"Titans", "patient as Sisyphus, powerful as Samson"— coexist with the traces of the first mountain townships' ruins: "though they have never known aught but peace and health, they, in one lesser aspect at least, look like countries depopulated by plague and war" (*Israel Potter*, 1982, 4). To the eyes of the discriminating traveller, the lasting beauty of American strength and value becomes visible in a synthesis of nature and history, which, while supporting an Emersonian vision of human artifacts as organic to the soil, also shows signs of regressive decay and the ravages of war usually attached to the Old World scene. There is a possible parallel between the two worlds; the analogy is suggested in Trumbull's vindication, to be denied as outrageous. Such a parallel does not fail to qualify Emersonian nature: the "great purple dome of Taconic" is "the St. Peter's of these hills", a hawk "sallying from some crag" resembles "a Rhenish baron of old from his pinnacled castle".

The Berkshire landscape as a typical mid-nineteenth century American space is qualified by the "eccentric" parallel coexistence of two lines of meaning—Americanism as organic to the soil, and Americanism as decaying in time. Such a type generates another type:

> Nor could a fitter country be found for the birthplace of the devoted patriot Israel Potter . . .
>
> Such, at this day, is the country which gave birth to our hero: prophetically styled Israel by the good Puritans, his parents, since for more than forty years, poor Potter wandered in the wild wilderness of the world's extremest hardships and ills.
>
> How little he thought, when as a boy, hunting after his father's stray cattle among these New England hills, he himself like a beast should be hunted through half of Old England, as a runaway rebel. Or, how could he have dreamed, when involved in the autumnal vapors of these mountains that worse bewilderments awaited him three thousand miles across the sea, wandering forlorn in the coal-fogs of London. But so it was destined to be. This little boy of the hills, born in sight of the sparkling Housatonic, was to linger out the best part of his life as a prisoner or a pauper upon the grimy banks of the Thames (*Israel Potter*, 5; 6).

The title-character is born out of the descriptive logic: he is a type (a devoted patriot) because he is a parallel type to the landscape. This recognition is "poetically" invoked in the modern eyes of the travelling you, and "facts", such as a birthdate, or the precise time in history when Israel Potter becomes a rebel, a prisoner, or an exile, are of no concern.

The position of the narrator is particularly interesting here because it can help clarify Melville's "configuration" of the textual interpreter of the *Life*'s plot: the narrator invites a contemplation of the future doom of the type in the form of an anticipation, sustained by a substitution—the English scene for the American—and a shift of focus from the landscape to the character. What the reader is invited to behold is the destiny of a "he" that includes the previous "it". The "you", as the eccentric protagonist of the American landscape vision,

123

is now both excluded and confirmed in its visionary function, since the vision of Israel's story to come is presented within the parallel "beholding" of the omniscient narrator who anticipates it. The pact that links voice and reader is enlarged to include the need to recognize in the text the space and time through which the anticipation realizes itself, thus suggesting the possible transition to a common "we", as the subject that may share the "reading" of the text's realized present.

If we assume, as a point of view, that the novel's symbolic logic is oriented by the rewriting of a previous historical narration, *Israel Potter* presents itself as a fiction that, renouncing the illusion of representing history, is structured by the actualization of the process of reading a text of history. The represention of the past in the classic historical novel is made continuous with the narrator's present by the constant reminder of the time in between; Melville's method symbolically privileges the time in between, or to borrow again Ricoeur's definition, stresses the passage between "within-time-ness"—so convincingly represented by "scenes" of the past "witnessed" by readers and narrators in Scott's historical fictions—and the experience of "historicality" as the shared construction of the relations between past and present and eventually the future.

In one of *Billy Budd*'s frequent self-reflexive asides, the narrator posits indirection as the method by which the "deadly space between"—a quote from Thomas Campbell's "The Battle of the Baltic"—can be crossed. The remark is addressed to a reader whose "normal nature" may be the liability that prevents his understanding of Claggart's own nature, or the understanding of the relation between "knowing the world" and "knowing human nature" (Melville, 1984, 1382). The awareness of the in-betweenness carries with it the mysterious role that deeper psychology plays in the interpretation of wordly events, or of the "reading" of history as interpretation. In *Israel Potter* Melville does not pry into his characters' "obscure spiritual places", but shapes his "eccentric reader" by soliciting a variety of psychological responses to the text, from laughter to tears, thus constructing the expectation of a personal catharsis.

When anticipations of Israel's destiny are realized in London, in the penultimate chapter of the novel, the variety of narrative modes has come to include lyrical description, comic picaresque adventures, gothic thrills, satire, epic, and pathos. The reader's desire for resolution—generated by symbolic method and by multiplicity of styles (Pagnini, 1970, 93-94)—is acknowledged when the time of the story is contracted near the end. The beholding function is accordingly turned into a collective "we" who has "seen" it all and is ready for a transition announced by: "we too cross over and skim events to the end". The narration of Israel's exile is rushed to conclusion: the "realism" of Israel's hardships in London is of no concern (Matthiessen, 1941, 491). The content of the anticipation (Israel's exile in London) is not expanded upon, but contracted. In such contraction the earlier parallel to the Berkshires is beheld again: "[B]ack to New England our exile was called in his soul" (164). The "alien" Israel who "looks" like a "trespassing Pequod Indian . . . long ago", hallucinating in St. James' Park, allows a Dickensian urban scene to trespass into the lyrical space of his childhood, and he actually herds his father's ghostly "stray cattle" into Barbican. The historical character's anticipated destiny is symbolically matched by a hallucination in which Israel's "future in the past" is realized in the reader's present in the pathos of an equally hallucinated "return of the same", which carries with it both realization and un-realization of the symbolic meaning of his type, a segment of the Berkshires and the exile from his country.

Israel's realized miseries are listed in summary-catalogues; one of them is an injury that caused him to limp, "excluding activity for no small part of the future, [and] was an added cause of his prolongation of exile" (162). Israel's limp, a fact from history reported in the syntagm of the "authentic" source, suggests that the exile to which it is connected is the symbolic configuration of the intersection between the syntagm and paradigm of his story. It is this intersection that is expanded upon in the novel, thus representing the coexistence of a sequentially certain destiny in which exile is a point of view in time—as suggested by anticipations—and its symbolic configuration—as Melville's "writing in" his reading of the source. Progression is contracted and stasis prolonged by the repetition of realization and unrealization of Israel's "historical exile". Exile is the privileged symbol of the potential merger of the narrator and reader's interpretative functions, or, metanarratively, the symbol of the historical narration as a reading process.

A symbolic configuration could be described as the suspension of resolution of parallels that share analogies, while still differing from each other. Yury Lotman defines parallelism as the concept in which "analogy rather than identity or separateness is stressed", since "one of its members is known through a second one that functions as an analogue in relation to the first, nor is separate from it. It is a state of analogy having those common features which are isolated in the recognition of the first member" (Lotman, 1976, 88). In this sense, a reading of "The Whiteness of the Whale"—Melville's monument to symbolism—would yield evidence for the workings of parallelism in a symbolic construction. Pure analogies in the opposite semantic fields of white as "good" and as "evil" are set side by side, paralleled: the logic of parallelism can thus both forward the suspension of identity and expand the possible range of unexpected analogies between opposites.

As a novel that reads an authentic text of history and symbolically parallels it in its re-writing, *Israel Potter* makes history the equivalent of the White Whale: its configuration as symbolic exile all but intensifies its value as a subjective epistemological inquiry. Considering the source as a parallel text, its historical characters and syntagm of events acquire their "literariness" in the segments they are made to share in new parallels with Nature, ideal national types and course of history; by the recurrent play of their imperfect analogies the novel historicizes anew the time in-between of un-realization as "our exile" or the exile of the nation from itself in the present of both reader and narrator.

It is a matter of speculation why Melville would have so quaintly recorded in his *Journal* Potter's autobiography as "the revolutionary narrative of the beggar" and whether he was not instead alluding to his own novel as "a revolutionary narrative". Be that as it may,

Melville's novel nonetheless shows the change from representational to symbolic in historical narrations and turns the reader-beholder into a new historical type whose function is determined by the parallelism between reading and configuring anew a text of history. Previous closures give way to an open process of interpretation, both claiming analogy with historically "authentic", "realized" representation and also departing from such representation by creating further analogies where similarity can be seen in opposites which the source conveyed as "false" and "unrealized". To extend the comparison with *Moby Dick*, in *Israel Potter* revolution becomes equivalent to the whale's whiteness; the revolution qualifies the exile as the permanence of revolutionary un-realized meaning, and, at the same time, makes the leviathan of national history unique.

The most insistent parallels in the novel involve characters as revolutionary types. This is not surprising since Melville chooses an "allegorical" strategy of characterization, and his first type, Israel, is introduced as a parallel to a representative American space and time. This type's valuable traits are substantially analogous to Trumbull's character, yet differ in one important detail. Giving the lie to Melville's own *Journal* entry, the narrator comments: "And here it might be noted, as a fact nationally characteristic, that however desperately reduced at times, even to the sewers, Israel, the American, never sunk below the mud, to actual beggary" (165). Trumbull's rhetoric of begging highlights the counterpositions between realized begging and false imposture, and between begging and a claim for reward justified by authentic Revolutionary action and valor. Israel's type takes on the disguise of the "beggar's garb" (153), he is no beggar, and no impostor. Denying beggary from his source, and in such a strong way (a national characteristic), Melville expels the only apparently un-American trait of his protagonist and gives him a heroic moral value that realizes a continuity from the Puritans to the Revolutionary Fathers. Exile is consequently qualified by an all-American paradigm of value confirmed by the Revolution. Americans are no beggars, as Franklin would say; neither are they rebels.

This is a national characteristic whose origin may be found in Cotton Mather's *The Wonders of the Invisible World* (1693). William Carlos Williams quotes the passage from Mather in his twentieth century meditation on national cultural paradigms:

> And a famous Person returning hence [from New England], could in a Sermon before the Parliament, profess "I have now been seven Years in a Country, where I never saw one Man drunk, or heard one oath sworn, or beheld one Beggar in the Streets all the while" (Williams, 1956, 82-3).

Cotton Mather intended such British reports to support his statement that New England was the type of "a real Utopia"; it remains a real utopic land in Israel's hallucinations. Not differently from Trumbull's strategy of vindication in the begging episode, the permanence of value reinforces its historical import in the community of readers, who may see in it the persistent legacy from the past, made dramatic by denial.

The denial of beggary is connected to an almost identical passage in the source and in Melville's text:

> as thirty years before, on all sides, the exile had heard the supplicatory cry, not addressed to him: "An honorable scar, your honor, received at Bunker-Hill, or Saratoga, or Trenton, fighting for his most gracious Majesty, King George!" So now, in the presence of the still surviving Israel, our Wandering Jew, the amended cry was anew taken up, by a succeeding generation of unfortunates . . . (165).

Melville "amends" the cry from the source, by adding Bunker Hill to the list of battles, by making his type an object of observation of the onlooking we, and by introducing an analogy lacking in Trumbull's text: "our Wandering Jew". Three new parallels are the result of the emendation: Napoleonic wars and American Revolution, Israel the agent and the revolutionary type under scrutiny, and Israel the all-American and the Wandering Jew. In the perspective of these new parallels, Israel, as the representative of his country, acquires a historical analogy with European revolutionary history and a moral difference (he is no beggar); a textual analogy between his action in history and its contemplation by common scrutiny; and finally a literary analogy with the topos of a destiny protracted by repetition.

Displaced in time (1775-1817) and in space (Berkshires—Europe), Israel's unbeggarly value is historicized "globally" by the parallel to resonant, international, "revolutionary" battles, while the historical man is doomed in the future by the plot-rule of a literary topos that encloses teleological movement in the stasis of repeated actions.

Israel's exile apparently starts with the Revolution; by symbolic logic the Revolution acquires the status of the exile's defining paradigm. Sustained revolutionary action is represented in the plot in the picaresque actions of the first chapters and more appropriately in the epic battle of the *Bon Homme Richard*. Yet inaction and repetition characterize the course of the hero's story. By that contrast with inaction, revolutionary action is suspended. Action stops in Franklin's house.

Within the syntagm of Israel Potter's story, the source only mentions in passing the protagonist's visit to Franklin in the Latin Quarter, whereas in the novel, besides marking a long pause in revolutionary action, this visit becomes the cause for the plot's turning point. Through Franklin's intervention Israel runs toward both his last revolutionary battle, and the realization of the Wandering Jew's destiny. In Franklin's house the revolutionary paradigm as global, moral, exiled value is contemplated in a prolonged confrontation of revolutionary types. Israel's "bottom nature" of American revolutionary everyman is exposed to the type of revolutionary politics (Franklin), and revolutionary action (John Paul Jones) and shares some segments of each parallel type: with Franklin, the Yankee cunning and spirit of enterprise; with Jones, the traits of heroism and revolutionary daring. Tellingly, Israel's second revolutionary battle as Jones's best man is as historically resonant as Bunker Hill, repeating Israel's action of valor but also his imprisonment. With a difference: now Israel's destiny can be seen as tragic. His heroic actions drive him to the "City of Dis", to his being called a "ghost" by the British master-at-arms, led to "no end in the world", or as the officer adds, "I keep leading him about because he has no final destination" (140).

The metaphysical import of this sentence has often been pointed out; in the logic of textual parallelism with the source, it shows the historical outcome of its rhetoric of vindication (Israel's unrewarded death); in the logic of revolutionary parallelism it is analogous to Franklin's own representative preoccupation for the "final destination" of his country during the Revolution. The satire of Franklin's advantageous, progressive plans for the course of history fills the time-in-between the syntagm of the source and the paradigm of revolutionary value to be vindicated once again in the present of reader and narrator.

Israel is kept a "captive" in Franklin's house, and is forced to transform his captivity into a passive time of learning; the "man of wisdom" characteristically distills words of wisdom into Israel's ears, thereby fortifying the *Life*'s traits of honesty and patriotism, but also of frugality and respectful language; yet from Franklin, Israel learns that planning and disguise are the arts through which national ideals can be realized in the future. The first prolonged description of "the Renowned Sage, Dr. Franklin" deserves to be quoted in full:

> Wrapped in a rich dressing-gown—a fanciful present from an admiring Marchesa—curiously embroidered with algebraic figures like a conjuror's robe, and with a skull-cap of black satin on his hive of a head, the man of gravity was seated at a huge claw-footed old table, round as the zodiac. It was covered with printed papers; files of documents; rolls of MSS; stray bits of strange models in wood and metal; odd-looking pamphlets in various languages; and all sorts of books; including many presentation copies; embracing history, mechanics, diplomacy, agriculture, political economy, metaphysics, metereology, and geometry. The walls had a necromantic look; hung about with barometers of different kinds; drawings of surprising inventions; wide maps of far countries in the New World, containing vast empty spaces in the middle, with the word D E S E R T diffusely printed there, so as to span five-and-twenty degrees of longitude with only two syllables,—which printed word however bore a vigorous pen-mark, in the Doctor's hand, drawn straight through it, as if in summary repeal of it; crowded topographical and trigonometrical charts of various parts of Europe; and geometrical diagrams, and endless other surprising hangings and upholstery of science (38-9).

Franklin's old, alchemic, necromantic traces are contiguous with the catalogue of new systems of knowledge; such disorder is transformed by a "vigorous" act of will into a political asset that still combines a conjurors's spirit with the plan of a world where the abridgement of the American desert and the crowded geography of Europe are set side by side. The "claw-footed old table"—which Melville was subsequently to transform in the apple-tree table's "three cloven feet", the symbol for Cotton Mather, his troublesome "science" and the *Magnalia Christi Americana* (*The Apple-Tree Table*, 1856)—is "round as the zodiac", a reference to Franklin's almanacs, but also a suggestion of the totality of the doctor's project. The segments of the Old World-ravage parallel contained in the Berkshires description are prolonged into his "summary repeal" of the "wilderness" and of its culturally organic trait. Accordingly Franklin's "European" side is stressed, as he is portrayed as a cosmopolitan American "wrapped" in a rich-dressing gown, the gift of an "admiring Marchesa". Aristocratic dressing gowns and urban middle-class (or revolutionary?) skull-caps adorn, in another striking new contiguity, the Yankee man of science; the former business man and present politician, paradoxically "disguises" himself in his public appearances with his native garments: a "tattered wardrobe" or a "linsey woolsey".

"[H]aving weighed the world, he could act any part in it": "printer, postmaster, almanack maker, essayist, chemist, orator, thinker, statesman, humorist, philosopher, parlor-man, political economist, professor of housewifery, ambassador, projector, maxim-monger, herb-doctor, wit". This Whitmanesque catalogue of modern social functions in one man parallels Israel's forced changes of garments and roles in his attempts to escape imprisonment (from that of a squire to those of an old ditcher, a scarecrow, a farm laborer, an impressed English sailor), and anticipates the contemporary narrative of *The Confidence Man—His Masquerade* (1857). Franklin—who ludicrously speaks in the echo of his own maxims, and gives *Poor Richard's Almanack* to Israel, together with a map of Paris, since "in this world, men must provide knowledge before it is wanted"—realizes in the past a consistent segment of Melville's present, by teleologically planning it.

Israel's English "desert" to come, appears in his home as the map of the American wilderness crossed out in Melville's time, one surmises, by Greeley's "go West, Young man", and by the realization of Franklin's own belief in the peopling of America by supporting immigration from European countries, a situation which was becoming a troubling issue of containment in the 1850s (Higham, 1981).

The contiguity between the American and the European space of Franklin's maps suggests, moreover, a possible solution to the official rhetoric of opposition to the Old World that construes American national identity through difference, claiming the uniqueness and supremacy of its principles. It is this rhetoric, characteristic also of Trumbull's *Life*, which is paralleled by Melville's first description of the American landscape. In the novel, the French and the English historical scenes "parallel" the American; France is on the verge of its own Revolution, and in England the principles of monarchic conservation and democratic innovation are battling with each other—as shown by Israel's earlier confrontation with the King (ch. 5) and with the English supporters of the American cause (ch. 6). Parallelism can become a radical act against the American isolationist and nativist impulse, while at the same time it may project the revolutionary American periphery, awakening to its Manifest Destiny, within the Western perspective of the nations which at mid-century still represented the center. In this, as before, Franklin is both the type of the plan and of the realization of the future in the past.

In the narrator's words Franklin's "white hair and mild brow spoke of the future as well as the past" (39): his real age does not matter, since he embodies the "exile" in American history's teleology, while standing for historical realization. As the current "type and genius of his land", he nearly becomes the American anti-type who, by imposing an imperfect new order to the revolutionary heroic "barbarism" of Ethan Allen and John Paul Jones, leads everyman's native traits to no "final destination".

Israel's doom or his "final destination" is anticipated at least three more times in the novel (19; 153; 160). It is coupled each time with the same semantic choices—displaced space, pauperism, imprisonment, and failure—which, as critics have noticed (see, for example, Berthoff, 1962; Frederick, 1962), stand for Melville's pessimistic attack on his country's history. Such repeated anticipations also function as an increasingly tragic denial of progression and as a reminder of the vindication's "historical" necessity. Accordingly these anticipations are being realized in the encounter with Franklin and suspended by the parallel encounter, in the man of wisdom's house, with John Paul Jones, the type of Revolutionary action.

It is Franklin who introduces Jones to Israel. In the Melvillean code of valor Jones stands high since he is presented as the type of the "untramelled citizen and sailor of the universe"; he is also a barbarian dandy, the very embodiment of the reckless spirit of the Revolution. As such, Jones establishes a false parallel between himself and Franklin; ironically he believes that they share the quality of being true: "You . . . are true, and deep; and so you are frank". This may sound like a pun on the national Father's name, Frank-lin, a belittling of revolutionary values, while representing them, a follow-up of Melville's satire; or it may sound like a false recognition that dooms Jones's true value in analogy with Israel's. And, as an apparent extension of Jones's false recognition, Israel is not able to detect false from true in Franklin's words and actions.

Like Hawthorne's Hutchinson in "Edward Randolph's Portrait", Israel is a bad reader of signs: in this he is the parallel opposite of Melville's configuration of the reader's type. In *Israel Potter*, as in "Benito Cereno", the reader is expected to see that the character does not see, and discover the "pleasure" of reading through the character's myopia (Cabibbo, 1983, 8). In contrast to Hawthorne's Hutchinson, Israel does not fail because he resorts to an inadequate system of knowledge (Franklin's *Poor Richard's Almanack*) but rather because he is not allowed to see: his sight is seriously impaired while he lodges in Franklin's rooms in Paris. This house of history and of its exile, where the paradigm of Revolution is explored, American types are brought together, the past is absorbed into the present, and the Old and New World are set side by side, is entered by Israel *after* "crossing the stone bridge over the *Seen*"—a bridge he would never cross again, since as Franklin promptly corrects him, he is bridging not the "Seen", but the Seine. Closeted by his host, he does not see the "wonders" of Paris, which the narrator's eye instead finds bristling with new scientific experiments and revolutionary preparations. When he is admitted to the sage's presence, Israel can not even see his face (Franklin's back "was turned to him"); his vision of the doings that follow there is indirect (through mirrors), or partial (through cracks of doors shut on him). "This is poor sight-seeing" indeed, as he himself comically remarks.

The comedy on Israel's reduced sight is followed by a gothic entombment from which he escapes in the garments of a "ghost". It is as a ghost that his sight comes back to him, before he is led away as a ghost with no final destination, and reappears as a hallucinating ghost in the London fogs. The view of an English landscape "magically reproduced to our adventurer, the aspect of Bunker Hill, Charles River, and Boston town, on the well remembered night of the 16th of June" (76). As repeatedly happens in the novel, it is the ghostly sight of a historically significant frozen time and frozen space that signals Israel's type of continuity in American history from the Puritans to the Revolution (Bunker Hill and the Berkshires). Through Franklin's intervention, the intersection between paradigm and syntagm of American history shows the perverted destination of the revolutionary Israel. His character cannot see the revolutionary un-realization of his present, though he himself is a revolutionary agent.

Israel does not see, however, what the novel's reader is made to read: that his type also embodies a tragi-comic parallel to the mid-century American everyman, whose vision of the present, a frozen image of the Revolution and the blindness to its possible ghastly perversion, can be figured as the static compound of the exile that dooms the future. To the eccentric reader who reads this last parallel, Franklin's realization of the revolutionary spirit that Jones embodies cannot speak for the future. Found lacking in the romantic function essential to the representation of the modern universe—"he was everything but a poet"—Franklin should be seen undisguised, "face to face". The reader's response to satire orients the interpretation of the time in between past and present towards the recognition of the moral value of the search for revolutionary realization.

In this quest the persistence of the exile can be turned into a time of value for the future that casts the past of the Revolution as its moral antecedent. The unrealized past of its "book"—constantly recalled for the reader by the repeated anticipations—symmetrically evokes the urge to overcome the stalled present with a projection into the future. Twice, after the satire of the Franklin chapters, are readers confronted with prophetic utterances and are thus configured as types of futurity. Dramatically obscure, the shared prophecies about the national future point to the moral vindication of "our exile", by renewing the meaning of revolution.

THE POLITICAL MESSIAH IS IN US

Both Melville and Hawthorne share a concern with the "authenticity" of shared vision. In Hawthorne's *Legends* the stress is on the comprehensiveness of a narration of history that incorporates sundry effects, and the narrator's voice is often one of doubt and possibility; in Melville's *Israel Potter*, effects are activated in the configuration of a communal reading process, oriented by the narrator's voice both towards catharsis and divination. Two different political orientations seem to be at stake: for Hawthorne the narration is "true" when the future can account for the past; for Melville the discourse of history is true when the future vindicates the past: in this his primary source is an "authentic" text of history.

In light of Hawthorne's American Claimant manuscripts the two orientations can be seen as complementary. For Hawthorne, however, to see the past "anew" excludes prophecy; the future is constructed in the present of an almost "analytical" individual relation to the past. As the spiritual Clifford says in his "electric" train conversation: "the past is but a coarse and sensual prophecy of the present and the future" (Hawthorne, 1983, 575) and modern mediums can do better. Still, as Richard Brodhead has convincingly argued, Melville's "notion of literature as a prophetical activity" appears to originate in his reading of "Hawthorne and His Mosses". It is Melville's own interpretation of the older writer's work as that of a "diviner" that, according to Brodhead, reveals the change in Melville's poetics at the end of the 1840s (Brodhead, 1986, 26-29). For Melville prophecy becomes a form of value, the vehicle of the potential renewal of the promise of history and of its Apocalypse. Melville's claim to the future is more grandiose, and more explicitly political than Hawthorne's: both, however, suggest a concern with plausible solutions for the rediscovered presence of the past in the forms of the modern. While the secular Hawthorne focuses on the morality of an individual process of "seeing" the past, the God-fearing Melville evokes a morality of history supported by Christian teleology. Still for both Hawthorne and Melville the past is a progressive and regressive force projected on the historical present.

In *Israel Potter* the narrator hoaxes readers with anticipations which refer to the chronology and the events of the source: "but here we anticipate a page" he says, in the transition between one expansion to another (ch.22-3). And to make the irony structural, Melville's own representation of the Revolution, another conspicuous departure from the source, is thus introduced:

> Elsewhere than here the reader must go who seeks an elaborate version of the fight, or, indeed, much of any regular account of it whatever. The writer is but brought to mention the battle, because he must needs follow, in all events, the fortunes of the humble adventurer whose life he records. Yet this necessarily involves some general view of each conspicuous incident in which he shares (120-1).

An excellent reader, Walt Whitman, the prophetic seer, did penetrate Melville's hoax when he incorporated much of *Israel Potter*'s battle, including two factual details of Melville's invention, in sections 35 and 36 of "Song of Myself" (Flibbert, 1974). Whitman turned his borrowing into a prophecy of revolutionary realization. In the 1855 edition of *Song*, it is not a "he", as in the later versions, but the poet's self who takes up an Israel Potter-like persona as the observer-participant of the battle, in a celebration of cameraderie with its captain, of Revolutionary valor and convulsed death, ending—as it does in Melville's novel—with the representative everyman imprisoned: "in prison shaped like any other man". By contrast Whitman's self breaks free of Israel's shackles and lack of final destination, and rises as a cosmic democratic force from his plunge into revolutionary history. As the 1855 preface to *Leaves of Grass* emphatically propagandizes:

> The attitude of great poets is to cheer up slaves and horrify despots . . . Come nigh them awhile and though they never speak or advise you shall learn the faithful American lesson. Liberty is poorly served by men whose good intent is quelled from one failure or two failures or any number of failures, or from the casual indifference or ingratitude of the people . . . Liberty relies upon itself . . . and knows no discouragement. The battle rages with many a loud alarm and frequent advance and retreat . . . the enemy triumphs . . . the prison, the handcuffs, the iron necklace and anklet . . . and is liberty gone out of place? No never (Whitman, 1982, 17).

Whitman's long catalogue of apparent attacks levelled against freedom closes with the prophecy that liberty, the native trait of "the American character", will not only survive the attacks, but triumph over the still pervasive "swarms of cringers, suckers, doughfaces, lice of politics . . . " (18).

With Walt Whitman, *Israel Potter* shares the method of a "political" transition from literality to figurality, from history to type and parallel. This transition is organized at crucial junctures into a prophetic discourse which projects into the future the particular both as universal and peculiarly American. In the parallel with the mock-serious strategy of anticipation in *Israel Potter*—as a rewriting of its historical source—prophecy, the figure of a discourse projected into the future, stands for the moral vindication of history. The form of prophecy comprehends the parallel-opposites of teleology and repetition of the same, and projects them into the future; the narrative logic of anticipation—as the certain expectancy of historical realization—is paralleled by a prophetic logic that both confirms teleology and suspends the time of realization. In between teleology and realization, there are man's uncertain ways of turning teleological certainties into historical action.

While Whitman prophesies, and vindicates the past, in the name of a "certain" future—transcending and cutting short its historical realization—Melville is aware of dramatic implications: national history is dramatized within a prophetic vision of the future that imperfectly contains the static tension caused by the new and necessarily open or "revolutionary" parallelism between New World geography and Old World scenes, opportunities and pauperism, freedom and slavery.

In *Israel Potter* both prophecies of the destiny of America are delineated by two revolutionary heroes, Ethan Allen and John Paul Jones. Allen, a frenzied man in British chains, is seen as a native rebel:

> His spirit was essentially Western; and herein his peculiar Americanism; for the western spirit is, or will yet be (for no other is or can be) the true American one (149).

John Paul Jones, the barbarian dandy, is "the prophetical ghost, glimmering in anticipation upon the advent of those tragic scenes of the French Revolution which levelled the exquisite refinement of Paris with the blood-thirsty ferocity of Borneo" (63). As a figure paralleling Queequeg (a "George Washington cannibalistically developed"), he animates the first revolutionary naval collision:

> There would seem to be something singularly indicatory in this engagement. It may involve at once a type, a parallel and a prophecy. Sharing the same blood with England, and yet her proved foe in two wars; not wholly inclined at bottom to forget an old grudge: intrepid, unprincipled, reckless, predatory, with boundless ambition, civilized in externals but a savage at heart, America is, or may yet be, the Paul Jones of nations (120).

These prophecies of the American future have been variously interpreted as a prefiguration of the Civil War, a belief in the frontier as the true paradigm of American history, or a critique of the Western World, as embodied by the Roman Empire, leading to a critique of American Imperialism (Karcher, 1980; McWilliams, 1984; Fussell, 1965; Bezanson, 1982; Dekker, 1987). Each of these interpretations is possible to a late twentieth-century reader. By definition, prophecies invite later readers to historicize the prophetic content within their knowledge of the course that followed.

Prophetic utterances are an intriguing presence in Melville's fiction—from those that prophetically parallel the American scene with the exotic lands and peoples in *Mardi*, and those that ominously foretell the fate of the Pequod in *Moby Dick*, to those that similarly cast a shadow on Pierre's happy youth. Rowland Sherrill has extensively examined Melville's prophetic forms on the premise that, at its best, Melville's aim was to suggest reformistically that "his prophetic speaking in fictive forms could be effectual, and, therefore, that changes of cultural perception were possible" (Sherrill, 1979, 3). Following Melville's increasing doubts and the consequent development of his transcendental pessimism, Sherrill omits *Israel Potter* from his investigation. Though this omission is not at all uncommon in critical discourse until the 1980s, it is nonetheless a noticeable missing link in Sherrill's argumentation, since *Israel Potter* represents the high point of Melville's poetic "reformative thrust" in history, historical outcomes (Civil War, expansionism) notwithstanding.

A first evidence for this is the textual position of the prophecies. Since they appear after the Franklin chapters, they can be seen as the form of the opposition to the Franklinian method of shaping revolutionary time by advantageous, finalistic "planning". Franklin is no more a prophet in the novel, than is the speaking voice in Trumbull's *Life*. Melville's almost identical use of verbs and tenses in the two prophetic passages links the present of America ("is") with the past of its revolutionary men and with its uncertain future, loaded with qualifications from the Revolution which become noticeably fearful in the second prophecy. In their obscurity, both prophecies are grounded in parallels with two characters embodying rebellion, barbarism, recklessness, and ambition. Since both are Revolutionary heroes the prophetic projection of their traits and actions into the future of the nation, shows that the Revolutionary paradigm—as the parallel between "barbarism" and "civilization"—is still the working paradigm for American historical self-definition, responsible for its "exile", as well as for its "solution" in the future.

Consistent with the description of the Berkshires, the future is cast as both organic to soil (frontier) and possibly bound to decay compared to "civilized" English imperial ways. Barbarism and civilization are not opposites—in terms of the historical and geographical divide between the American West and the European World—but rather parallels that share both negative and positive segments of meaning: a constructive and destructive thrust coexist in both as heroic vision and transformation, as ruthless appropriation and sinful regression.

The prophetic mood is, of course, the romantic way of dealing with controversial historical truths: in Scott's novels it is activated mainly within the gloomy sphere of the supernatural, in the prophecies of revenants (see *Waverley*) or weird characters (like Meg in *The Bride of Lammermoor*), or it is even parodied (*The Talisman*). In James Fenimore Cooper's *The Last of the Mohicans*, prophecy is the form of utterance of the Indians, the vehicle of a universalist type of continuity between the red and the white races (Cagidemetrio, 1989). It is with Thomas Carlyle's *The French Revolution* (1837) that prophecy signally becomes a function of the historical narrator contemplating the Revolution as a paradigm of self-definition. Carlyle's method of dealing with his own historical sources is to project their pastness into the future of the events he relates. Anticipating the outbreak of the Revolution in his chapter "Realized Ideals" (Book I), the narrator resorts to a long quote of the description of a 1750 dramatic riot from one of his sources and concludes:

> "Some of the rioters", adds Lacretelle, quite coolly, "were hanged the following days;" the Police went on. O ye poor naked wretches! and this then is your inarticulate cry to Heaven, as of a dumb tortured animal, crying from uttermost depths of pain and debasement? Do these azure skies, like a dead crystalline vault, only reverberate the echo of it on you? Respond to it only by "hanging on the following days"?—Not so; not for ever! You are heard in Heaven. And the answer too will come,—in a horror of great darkness, and shakings of the world, and a cup of trembling that all nations shall drink (Carlyle, 1989, 1, 14).

Through a rhetoric of interrogation, Carlyle's narrator combines the impulse to share the exegesis of the historical text with his readers, with the answer to it, the spirit of prophecy. This prophecy relies on the knowledge of the Revolution as a fact of history, but it is cast in the recurrent metaphorical language of an interpretation of its "realized ideals". Prophetic utterance is for Carlyle the rhetorical figure that answers his own generation's struggle between order and disorder, articulate and inarticulate, which is, to him, the valuable and lacerating struggle of modernity the revolutionary paradigm contains.

"We are dealing not with historical curiosity", Geoffrey Hartman writes of Carlyle's prose, "but with a creative historiographical act", with the representation of the actual "merging" between sources and commentary that makes the reader's role "explicit". Such prose, Hartman adds, had its almost unique counterpart in Melville's prose (Hartmann, 1986, 124-25). In *Israel Potter*, Melville's narrator, like Carlyle's, aims at a prophetic "visionary merger", thus abandoning the testimonial function of Scott's narrators who conveyed the illusion of a realization of the past in the present, an illusion propped up by the seemingly thorough faithfulness to authoritative sources of the past. Both Melville and Carlyle turn instead to a principle of arbitrary selection of sources (Melville writes that he chanced upon the *Life*) and to the exhibition of their exegetical drive as a preliminary for prophecy. While Hawthorne underplays Carlyle's prophetic utterances, privileging instead the new "representational" quality of *The French Revolution*, Melville retains a narratorial obsession with rhetorically collective claims, thus configuring in the reader-narrator "merger" a shared cultural imperative formulated in *White-Jacket* as: the political Messiah "has come in *us*" (Melville's underlining).

Both Carlyle and Melville echo the book of *Revelation*. For Carlyle the "end of history" of *Revelation* resonates in the representation of the Revolution, and the promise of *Revelation* resonates in the "constructive" thrust of narratorial prophetic utterances. In *Israel Potter* the "final destination" passage comes *after* the Revolution, as the "end of history", has been represented in the epic and tragic naval clash, and in between the two prophetic utterances. To stress once more the impact of Melville's reading of Carlyle in 1850 (Sealts, 1988), the prophetic configuration of *Israel Potter* can be seen as inspired by another passage oriented by the language of *Revelation* from *Sartor Resartus*, in which its fictitious German source is retailored by a question-answer commentary:

> Whence? How? Whereto? The answer lies around, written in all colours and motions, uttered in all tones of jubilee and wail, in thousand figured, thousand-voiced, harmonious nature; but where is the cunning eye and ear to whom the God-written Apocalypse will yield articulate meaning? We sit as in a boundless Phantasmagoria and Dream-grotto (Carlyle, 1969, 1, 41).

Melville is not interested, as Hawthorne was, in Carlyle's phantasmagorias, but in the questionings of a would-be prophetic subjectivity. The British officer asks Israel, the survivor of the revolutionary battle:

> Where did you come from? What's your business? Where are you stationed? . . . How did you get here? And where are you going? (137).

To the questions posed to "everyman" after the Revolution, *Revelation* both as God-written Apocalypse and promise of resurgence conveys the dramatic urgency of a prophet able to read through the "tones of jubilee and wail" and turn revolution into revelation. This is the cultural framework to which Emerson subscribed when he wrote in "Literary Ethics" (1838): "Since Carlyle wrote French History, we see that no history that we have is safe, but a new classifier shall give it new and more philosophical arrangement" (Emerson, 1983, 103). Emerson's call for the new "history" does not stress the drama of *Revelation*, but rather the centrality of the first person singular's interpretation as the possible "classifier" that could make history both new and meaningful within the collective enterprise of defining future America. "This country has not fulfilled what seemed the reasonable expectation of mankind" he says, since its brood of "Titans" has still not yielded the type of scholar whose "existence and pursuits would be a happy omen" even if the results of his labors "were incommunicable". Characteristically for Emerson, since there is no "safe" book of the past in the "new, untried world", the responsibility of connecting the past to the present is that of the "seer", whose process of seeing alone guarantees the future as a project of "the New", regardless of its clarity.

Melville's prophetic utterances subscribe to the earlier Carlyle-Emerson concept of the past as a project for the new uttered by a dauntless subject, the new Messiah upon which Whitman's self is also modelled. The insistence on a communal "we"—we the readers—makes the collectivity a post-revolutionary prophet, or a subjectivity of political value, whose moral concern is to bridge the gap between Christian teleology and historical stasis.

The modern concept of "future past", as Reinhart Koselleck has taught us, is never disjointed from the creation of a new subjectivity, a "collective singular" born out of the Revolution as a new start in history and as a metahistorical "regulative principle of knowledge". After the 1848 European revolutionary unrest, the idea of a "permanent" revolution began to emerge from the experience of both revolutionary time-acceleration and delayed historical realization (Koselleck, 1985, 46-7). Melville's prophecies can be seen as the poetic form which conveys the post-1848 renewed need for historical prediction in the contemporary historiographical discourse (Koselleck, 1985, 55-62) and the assessment of a delayed realization in history of revolution as a progressive paradigm of national self-definition. Paradoxically the "exile" of history, history's "inarticulateness", was becoming more apparent within the time acceleration brought about by contemporary events such as the Western expansion, and the Fugitive Slave Act, no less than the 1848 unrest. In such dramatic perspective revolution is seen again as the struggle between barbarism and civilization, while its value is turned "permanent" by resorting to the the collective moral responsibilty of the interpreter. Trumbull's 1824 *Life* recorded a "delayed realization" of revolutionary expectations and vindicated them in the certainties of the discourse of American history. *Israel Potter* vindicates revolutionary expectations by making them the collective permanent legacy of the past to be morally spent in an uncertain future.

In delineating Melville's "democratic merger", the "reformative thrust" in his revolutionary tale, *Israel Potter*'s companion piece, "Benito Cereno", should not be forgotten since it ironically reverses the morality of an American "reading" into a ludicrous failure of interpre-

tation. The novel and the tale are companion pieces, not only chronologically, but because both are exhibited "rewritings" of one source
(Sealts, 1988, 91). A comparison between the two works would
undoubtedly lend further evidence to the description of Melville's historical method in the fifties. To recall just a few of their common
strategies and to suggest their differences may be sufficient here.

In both texts "stasis" ("the long calms spoken of" in "Benito
Cereno"), is the locus of the tension between articulate and inarticulate, realization and its denial. The mock-realization of the beginning
"Seguid vuestro jefe" turns out to be the anticipation of the final
"Benito Cereno, borne on the bier, did, indeed, follow his leader".
Different yet analogous to the narrator-reader pact in *Israel Potter*, the
narrator does not evoke for the reader the possibility of a shared
vision, but insists on hypothetical suggestions (might, perhaps, etc.)
about the accuracy of the meaning of what is described. As if by
focusing the scene only through "the blunt-thinking American's
eyes", the narrator dramatizes the reader not as a new democratic
"eccentric" but as a stereotypical everyman who sees reality only by
referentiality (Materassi, 1983, 107). It is possible that "Benito
Cereno" gives "sight" back to the earlier type of Israel Potter and with
unsightly results. Carlyle's method of inducing a vision shared by
narrator and reader is mocked in Amasa Delano's constant questions
and ever faltering answers to his own questions, of which this is a
specimen:

> What was that which so sparkled? thought Captain Delano. It was no
> lamp —no match—no live coal. Could it have been a jewel? But how
> come sailors with jewels?—or with silk-trimmed undershirts either?
> Has he been robbing the trunks of the dead cabin passengers? But if
> so, he would hardly wear one of the stolen articles on board ship here.
> Ah, ah —if now that was, indeed, a secret sign I saw passing between
> this suspicious fellow and his captain awhile since; if I could only be
> certain that in my uneasiness my senses did not deceive me, then . . .
> (Melville, 1984, 697).

As the deposition from the source makes clear at the end, in this
instance Delano fails to discover a young nobleman by force disguised

as a sailor. It is the same sailor who, the deposition tells us, made one of the attempts to warn the American Captain of the ship's true condition. Historical evidence is used in "Benito Cereno" as the a-posteriori truth. This truth is subjectively both suggested and made elusive in the character's process of vision. As a consequence, narratorial prophetic utterances are excluded from this text.

Dwelling in the isolation of Delano's vision, Melville mocks *Israel Potter*'s prophetic method. The parallel invocation of the function of Emerson's individual historical genius—in "Literary Ethics"—seems to be mocked too:

> Think alone, and all places are friendly and sacred. The poets who have lived in cities have been hermits still. Inspiration makes solitude anywhere. Pindar, Raphael, Angelo, Dryden, De Staël, dwell in crowds, it may be, but the instant thought comes, the crowd grows dim to their eye; their eye fixes on the horizon,—on vacant space (Emerson, 1983, 105).

Delano's space as the space of the isolated American man remains insistently "vacant", the invocation and celebration of intervening, beneficient, native geniuses notwithstanding. The bleakness of "Benito Cereno" stems from insistent nonrealization, not from the parallel with realization, as in *Israel Potter*. The tale shows two different and opposed ways of writing history—the symbolic and the evidential— organized as a before and an after, while the novel dramatizes the configuration of the "evidence" of its source and gives new rhetorical form to the vindication of the past.

It could be maintained, following Eric Sundquist (Sundquist, 1986, 93-122), that the subject of the tale—the haunting presence in the collective historical consciousness of the Santo Domingo upheaval as a possible parallel to the potential insurgency of the American slaves—shuns prophecy. The Revolution, prophecy's true paradigm, is displaced. Americanism as a moral collective, revolutionary destiny can be expressed in the form of prophecy; the shadow of the Negro plausibly does not only cast a gloomy tinge over the course of history, but also generates a dumbing fear for the collective self. As Melville's opposition between evidence and vision testifies, a narrative relating the past and present of slavery with the national future was still to be "written" and could not be read (Placido, 1975, 90), or vindicated, as the revolutionary tale of Israel Potter is, by the invoked community of political messiahs.

THE UR-SOURCE OF NATIONAL PROPHECY

In more than one sense Melville's age is an age of prophecy. There is, however, a recognized American tradition of historical prophecy based on biblical exegesis which stemmed from the Old World's "Glorious Revolution", and which so vigorously flourished in the New World, where the early Puritans had planted it, that it imposed its language on subsequent, more secular, organic, romantic prophets.

Melville's method of "type, parallel and prophecy" in *Israel Potter* is the starting point of Ursula Brumm's own "typology" of the American "Calvinistic form" of symbolism (Brumm, 1970, 19). Brumm's concern is to differentiate between the American, and the European modern, symbolist traditions by stressing the opposite directions of theology and history pursued by the symbolic methods in the two cultures. While historicizing American symbolic techniques by linking them to Puritan thought, typology becomes, with Brumm, the ahistorical paradigm of American literature. Yet ahistorical paradigms do remain functions of history, as cultural formations that shape its narration and historically modify responses to reality.

As the work of Sacvan Bercovitch has shown, Puritan typology is both a fixed paradigm and a flexible discourse containing historical crises, adapting itself to the expression of critical insurgences. Melville's symbolism may be read as an "instance of the repudiation of historical thought" (Brumm, 1970, 195). As Reinhart Koselleck maintains, European post-Enlightenment historical thought repudiated typology in the name of descriptive "science", and substituted "accurate prediction" to prophecy (Koselleck, 1985, 3-72). In this, American romantic historians such as George Bancroft can speak for a different cultural orientation. The American discourse of history nonetheless remains an intertextual reference in literary works, which, as

Melville's work especially shows, is more relevant the more the "typology of the American Mission" is represented as jeopardized by historical "chaotic" forces.

As a reader of both the Bible and its historical exegesis, Melville configures *Israel Potter* with biblical analogues, intertextually matching the configuration of Trumbull's *Life* in "type, parallel, and prophecy". The historically authentic source is read through the ur-source of American historical discourse and is thus made its representative.

In Trumbull's *Life* only one biblical analogue has been detected (Wright, 1949); yet the very name of the character historicizes the presence of the Bible in the Revolution. Such coincidence between Bible and history is actually advertised in the novel's chapter headings—both a "synopsis and a prefiguration", where Israel's surname never appears (Cohen, 1991, 296-7). "Israel in the Lion's Den", "Samson among the Philistines", " . . . and Israel's Flight towards the Wilderness", and "Israel in Egypt" prepare us for "Forty-five Years", or Israel's exile which, as we are told at the beginning of chapter 25, "surpassed the forty years in the natural wilderness of the outcast Hebrews under Moses" (161), thus stressing, when the narrative is about to reach its end, the allusion contained in the title "His Fifty Years of Exile", minus the personal pronoun.

This suppression matches the different count of the years of Israel's exile. Fifty years elapse between 1776, the date of the Declaration of Independence, and Israel's homecoming, which Melville, differently from the source, sets in 1826. Israel falls into British hands and is carried off to England in 1775, as the novel reports. The biblical reference serves to cover the fifty years elapsed since the founding of the nation (celebrated in 1826).

While the novel's title and dedication present the text as a biographical account, the chapter headings' biblical analogies tightly connect Israel's personal story to the nation's God-approved teleology. As Emerson repeatedly said, "there is no History, but Biography", also adding:

Who cares what the fact was, when we have made a constellation of it to hang in heaven an immortal sign? London, Paris and New York must go the same way. "What is history," said Napoleon, "but a fable agreed upon?" ("History" [1836], 1983, 240).

Within *the* fable collectively agreed upon, the biblical interpretation of American history, Israel Potter's life proves that the fulfillment of the national prophecy to date since 1776 can be regressive. The national experience is turned backward and the Revolution joins the paradigm of the Puritan Great Migration: Israel, American born, is forced into becoming an immigrant to England ("Poor Israel! well-named—bondsman in the English Egypt"); his revolution is not a passage toward a better world but toward a worse one. His return to the Promised Land cannot but be doomed, because his imperfect sight is not compensated by a sacred sign from *Exodus* which would show the exile the way out of the London fogs ("In that London fog, went before him the ever-present cloud, but no pillar of fire by the night"). Israel's adventures do not end in the New Canaan he himself has been dreaming of, but in a "Potters' field", a symbolic final destination for biblical Israel no longer a prisoner in the English Egypt (Bianchi, 1990). Literally Potter's field is a graveyard on Copp's Hill facing Bunker Hill. It is the graveyard where both Increase and Cotton Mather are buried; in the Bible the "potter's field to bury strangers in" was bought, in fulfillment of Jeremiah's prophecy, with Judah's betrayal money, "Therefore that field has been called the Field of Blood" (Matthew, 27: 3-11).

As Sacvan Bercovitch has argued, post-revolutionary readers would look at the revolutionary past as "prophecy postdated" and at the future of the Revolution as "prophecy antedated". The origin of this concept of historical time is traced back to Nicholas Noyes' 1698 sermon on the American Errand, which declared: "prophesie is history antedated; and history is postdated prophecy" (Bercovitch, 1976, 15, 147). Melville had earlier ascribed to the political, post-revolutionary typology of the American Mission in this often quoted passage from *White-Jacket* (1850):

And we Americans are the peculiar, chosen people—the Israel of our time; we bear the ark of the liberties of the world. Seventy years ago we escaped from thrall; and, besides our first birth-right—embracing one continent of earth—God has given to us, for a future inheritance, the broad domains of the political pagans, that shall yet come and lie down under the shade of our ark, without bloody hands be lifted. God has predestinated, mankind expects, great things from our race; and great things we feel in our souls. The rest of the nations must soon be in our rear . . . Long enough have we been skeptics with regard to ourselves, and doubted whether, indeed, the political Messiah had come. But he has come in *us*, if we would but give utterance to his promptings. And let us remember that with ourselves, almost for the first time in the history of earth, national selfishness is unbounded philanthropy; for we can not do a good to America but we give alms to the world (Melville, 1983, 506).

Such celebration of Israel-America is dramatized even more radically than in *White-Jacket* in *Israel Potter*, starting with the chapter headings and the plot's reversal of the promise. Yet Israel as the type of the Puritan descendant and Revolutionary Father is a parallel—not identical—to the syntagm of regression.

Israel's personal catastrophic syntagm is only one side of the novel's parallel with national prophetic biography. In his germinal essay "How the Puritan Won the American Revolution", Sacvan Bercovitch assimilates, on the ground of the common rhetoric of the Jeremiad, a classically authoritative text of history such as George Bancroft's *History of the United States* with the "radical" works of the American Renaissance. These are works, Bercovitch maintains, which, though apparently attacking the present social status, make of the "unrepresented" Revolution the national paradigm of self-definition around which a subtler form of consensus can be articulated anew (Bercovitch, 1972). Bancroft's *History*—whose ten volumes oriented the reading of the national past from 1834 to 1876—"transmutes the colonial past into myth, and in epic form sets forth God's unfolding design for America, the revolution of revolutions that was born aboard the *Mayflower* and *Arbella* and matured in the struggles of 1776". Bancroft takes for granted the vindication of present continuity with the Founding Fathers, and weaves the national self-defining paradigm of revolution out of the "two quintessential moments in the story of America . . . the Great Migration and the War of Independence" (Bercovitch, 1972, 603-604).

Israel Potter too takes for granted the continuity between the Puritan and the Revolutionary fathers; its chapter headings suggest the same mythical movement that links migration to Revolution, at the same time inverting them in the parallel with antithetical types which act as agents of perversion. It can be surmised that the Revolution is both progressive and regressive: it regresses to the bondage prior to the Great Migration, yet it is progressive because it projects forward its passage to a better world.

Types of history are biblically reinterpreted in both directions: the revolutionary heroes, including Potter, share the prowess of David and the strength of Samson. It is the same strength of the American fore-fathers: "powerful as Samson" were the hardy Puritans that had cleared the wilderness of the New World and bounded it with their walls in the opening description of the Berkshires. "Neither is here wanting a biblical parallel" (46), the narrator says, introducing Franklin not as Benjamin but as Jacob, the name that God changed into Israel, and qualifies Franklin-Jacob as "a Machiavelli in tents", while the biblical progenitor was "a plain man living in tents" (Gen., 25: 7). Jacob cheats Israel out of his Puritan name and birthright (Zaller, 1976; Gilmore, 1977; for an opposite reading see Dillingham, 1986). The historical Benjamin is therefore substituted by a biblical Benjamin: it is Potter's son, "the spared Benjamin" of his father's old age, who does accomplish the passage out of the Egypt of his father's exile. In a bib-lical variant from the source it is the exiled Father who instills in the son the dream of *Exodus* (Cohen, 1991, 312): "the boy felt added longing to escape his entailed misery, by compassing for his father and himself a voyage to the Promised Land" (166). The English-born son is to perform anew the rite of passage that the actual Benjamin Franklin has historically reversed in the Revolution, turning the type of the father-descendant into a bondsman in the English Egypt.

Melville's extensive and intricate use of biblical parallels in *Israel Potter* has been variously noted as ironic, or uselessly overdone (Wright, 1949; Dryden, 1968), yet there seems to be more to it; his claim in the preface to *Israel Potter* that the novel's merit "must be in the general fidelity to the main drift of the original narrative" can also be read as the reassessment of Melville's own claim to tradition, to the "order" of the Puritan interpretation of the course of American history. When Israel Potter is entombed alive during his revolutionary mission as a spy for Franklin, the narrator links his entombment to similar ones from the Middle Ages to the Reform, to the times "of civil dissension". The historical parallel to Israel's own situation suggests a parallel with the book of Daniel: "With all this history ringing into his brain . . . At length, after what seemed the prophetic days and years of Daniel, morning broke" (71). It is the morning that will re-link Israel to the history of the American Revolution and of its battles. The Revolution as post-dated prophecy contained in earlier times of dissension is balanced against the Revolution as ante-dated to the early insurgent spirit of the Fathers.

If typology is "a form of prophecy which sets two successive historical events into a reciprocal relation of anticipation of fulfillment" (Brumm, 1970, 27), Melville's reader is left to confront the gap both between the Great Migration and Revolution (the interpretation of the colonial past) and between the Revolution and the present (the national past), and figure the direction of the present as in-between anticipation and fulfillment.

The reader's configuration as the biblical interpreter confirms national "exceptionalism" and the challenge to prove its authenticity. There is no doubt that Americans are constructed as prophets: the national biblical prophetic analogy in the political and historical discourse of his time is consistently paralleled throughout Melville's works (Heimert, 1963), and *Israel Potter* is no exception. Yet dealing with "Israel" as the apparent, exiled outcast of history, the text strongly suggests both the dramatic content of biblical prophecies and the ambiguity between prophetic truth and prophetic falsity.

Melville's own concern with biblical prophets is well known; in his copy of the *Holy Bible with Apocrypha* several underlinings and bracketings stress the ambiguity between "authentic" and "false" prophecy, like this passage in "The Lamentations of Jeremiah": [bracketing] "Thy prophets have seen vain and foolish things for thee: and they have not discovered thine iniquity, to turn away your captivity; but have seen for thee false burdens and causes of banishment" (2: 14; Cowen, 1987, 306); or this from Isaiah: "For this *is* a rebellious people, lying children, children *that* will not hear the law of the Lord: [bracketing] Which say to the seers, See not; and to the prophets, Prophesy not unto us right things, *speak unto us smooth things, prophesy deceits*" (30: 9-10; Cowen, 1987, 300). In the *New Testament*, the same concern appears again: "Wo unto you, when all men shall speak well of you! for so did their fathers to the false prophets" (Luke, 6: 26; Cowen, 1987, 325), or *"Sleep now and take your rest*: behold, the hour is at hand, and the son of man is betrayed into the hands of sinners", with the addition of an annotation "this is ironical" (Matthew, 24: 45; Cowen, 1987, 325).

Daniel is insistently referred to in the novel, as almost a textual figure both of dramatic content of prophecy and of an ambiguous true/false relation. The descendant of David, a captive exile in Babylon, an intrepreter of signs, delivered prophecies that as Calmet reports were considered unworthy to belong to the "canonical Scriptures" and were deemed by Porphyry "histories of past events", because of their exceeding historical accuracy (Calmet, 1832, 332). Both a prophet true to history and an historian false to prophecy, Daniel dominates the paradigm of revolution.

In "the lion's den", facing George III, still his king, Israel proves true to the democratic revolutionary God, thus invoking the parallel with Daniel, taming the antagonist British lion. Yet, like Daniel, Franklin too is "a lion tamer" who "might soothingly manipulate the aggravated king of beasts" (57). A historical figure false to prophecy, Franklin manipulates both Jones and Israel who share the appellative of lions when engaged in action (92; 102). In a variant of the apocryphal reference of the Queequeg-Ishmael encounter, soon after the introduction of John Paul Jones, Franklin, called to his diplomatic duties by the unexpected visit of two French aristocrats on an official mission, invites the barbaric hero both to conceal himself and to sleep with Israel, the descendant of the Puritans. The two do not lie together, since Jones paces the room and sleeps not; neither does Israel in bed, engaged as he is in looking at Jones' reflection in the mirror. What Israel is indirectly contemplating and unsuccessfully trying to make out, is the image of the revolution itself in Franklin's house. John Paul Jones, Franklin's savage guest, is prophetically said by the narrator to "possess a character as yet unfathomed and hidden power to back unsuspected projects", while "the heart of the metropolis of modern civilization was secretly trod" by this figure of revolutionary barbarism.

During his Babylonian captivity, in a sleepless night, Daniel, his face turned towards Jerusalem, sees the four beasts that were to ravage the earth before the advent of the kingdom of God. The first "was like a lion, and had eagle wings", and the fourth most gory and terrifying of all—supposedly the Roman Empire—had "a mouth speaking great things" (Daniel, 7: 8). In Daniel's prophecy, the knowledge of this last beast's true meaning is postponed until the kingdom of the Savior will be realized on earth. Yet the beast is described as one of violent appropriation "which shall devour the whole earth, and shall tread it down, and break it into pieces" (7: 23). The sleepless Israel, a Daniel in the House of Franklin, is set in the center of a static vision of the Revolution both as a thing of valor and a barbarian tattoo on the arm of Jones, a young David biblically both lion and eagle, lost in a "reverie" in front of the mirror. Israel is not able to decipher the tattoo's "large intertwisted cyphers", as he has not been able to read through the "mouth speaking great things" of Franklin, the lion tamer.

Besides wreaking havoc, Daniel's fourth beast causes a "change in time and laws" and "speaks *great* words against the most High" (7: 24). Daniel interprets the apocalyptic writings on the wall of Belshazzar's banquet hall (Daniel, 5), while comically Israel is not even able to decipher the word O-T-A-R-D; he must accept Franklin's translation—"poison"—and renounce his first practical Yankee impulse to find out by tasting it.

The seat of both the order and disorder of the Revolution, of both barbarism and civilization, the house in the Latin Quarter can be seen as the ambiguously stalled space between politics and action. It is also the space of Daniel, the space between the truth and falsity of American prophetic discourse; or symmetrically between the action that would prove the truth of the Revolution as a progressive stage in the national biblical destiny, and its parallel-opposite, a representation false to prophecy but politically deemed true. In this biblical suspension, Israel the nation appears as suspended between the two stages of its doing and undoing. False prophecy undoes the national potential, it is the "poison" of the words of Daniel's fourth beast. At the same time those words do not redeem but hide the barbaric gory destruction of beastly revolutionary action.

As Robert Zaller has noticed, for Melville revolution is "creative and benign" when it projects ad infinitum "a contiguity of opposites"; only the fusion of rebellion and assassination is invariably destructive (Zaller, 1976, 613). The myth of the Fathers' "bloodless revolution" enthralls Melville almost as much as Hawthorne was mesmerized by its opposite. Both, however, denounce the silence over the "killing" in the discourse of American history: Hawthorne with his unwashable "bloody stains", and Melville with his gory scenes of destruction. Still Melville's revolutionary destruction in *Israel Potter* is supported by the biblical parallel to a destruction containing purification: the *Bon-Homme-Richard* sinks in fire and water "like Gomorrah" out of sight (130). By analogy Franklin's political discourse is doomed, leaving behind the possibility of biblical resurrection by cataclysmic purification rituals performed by new Messiahs.

Christic references and their relation to the *Pilgrim's Progress* have been detected in *Israel Potter*'s symbolism (especially Rampersad, 1969); what is relevant here is the transition from the Old Testament to the New in the novel's symbolism, configuring God's predestination of the chosen people in the Messiah that has both come and has still to come.

In Melville's *New Testament* (1844) two passages are bracketed and underlined in Luke (13: 34-5) and Matthew (23: 37-8), respectively entitled: "Christ lamenteth over Jerusalem" and "The destruction of Jerusalem foretold".

> O Jerusalem, Jerusalem, *thou* that killest the prophets and stonest them which are sent unto thee, how often would I have gathered thy children together, even as a hen gathered her chickens under *her* wings, and ye would not! Behold, your House is left unto you desolate . . . (Matthew, 23: 37-8).

Luke does not differ from Matthew; the true prophets are still unrecognized and even stoned, and this both prevents the Messiah from "gathering" the people together and hastens the destruction of Jerusalem.

John's prophetic description of "the heavenly Jerusalem", or the New Jerusalem, after he witnesses the destruction of the Old is equally marked, by parallel lines:

> And I John saw the holy city, new Jerusalem, coming down from God out of heaven, prepared as a bride adorned for her husband. And I heard a great voice out of heaven, saying, Behold, the tabernacle of God *is* with men, and he will dwell with them, and they shall be his people, and God himself shall be with them, *and be* their God. And God shall wipe away all tears from their eyes; and there shall be no more death, neither sorrow, nor crying, neither shall there be any more pain: for the former things have passed away. And he that sat upon the throne said, Behold, I make all things new. And he said unto me, Write: for these words are true and faithful (*Revelation*, 21: 1-4).

The book of *Revelation* reinforces the symmetry between the *before* and the *after* of the event of true prophecy, and confirms the prophet as the voice of God, which invites the writing of the true book of the future.

The New Messiah is not the historical revolutionary type of the Father, but its addressee and descendant, the reader whose "experience of historicity" is the "visionary merger" of "us", the national community of readers. The *Life*'s vindication in history needs the configuration of the catastrophe in order to suggest the political truth of national resurgence, like "phenix from the ashes" as the unartful yet representative voice of Trumbull's Israel puts it.

In the copresence of regression and progression, destruction and resurgence, the story of a private soldier is rewritten into a symbolic national biography, that of an America of biblical resonance. While the democratic plea of such a transformation has been noticed many times, the peculiar resistance of "Americanness" and its own transformation has not received the same attention, especially from those critics who stress Melville's radical pessimism and historically catastrophic forebodings (Karcher, 1980, McWilliams, 1984). Yet Americanness is once again the mark of a special destiny and a new messianic political project. "Americanness" can be seen, as Bercovitch does, from inside the nation as the formulation of a unique middle-class compromise between historical contradiction and teleological belief. It can also be read from a point of view "outside" the nation as the paradigmatic formation of American postcolonial national identity.

Our own concern, as readers of the post-revolutionary generation of writers of the American Renaissance, inevitably leads us to define the peculiar national quality of these writers, by focusing on two foundational events, the Great Migration and the Revolution, which were being culturally "invented" anew in the first half of the nineteenth century. While the implications of this invention are multifarious and far-reaching, what seems pertinent in the reading of *Israel Potter*'s biblical intertextuality is the historical persistence and flexibility of its typological paradigm, which once again is cast as the "authentic" generative construct of national biography, unique because it is "sacrally" different. Difference and uniqueness carry with them the instability, not denial, of historical actualization.

To resort to the past, as has been often noted, implies facing both a disruption and a new continuity: the successful compromise must be measured in a geographical space and insurgent time which can be unified only in a symbolic space of nationality (Anderson, 1983). It is the "neutral ground" expected from the historical novel. In *Israel Potter*, the neutral ground is characteristically a function of the reader and is oriented by a biblical discourse which leaves to Benjamin, son of Israel's old age, to discern mythic Israel, the Canaan beyond the sea, in the symbolic space of the passage between the Old World and the New. It is a passage that obsessively denies and magnifies the Revolution as its equivalent. The American revolution is also the realization of the post-dated prophecy of the Old World insurgent Puritan Fathers as Potter's fancied old times of "civil dissention" suggest. The national symbolic space of New Canaan has to account for the immigrant Father's "exile" by figuring a parallel between it and the exile of the nation from itself—as if not England, but its biblical American counterpart, the English Egypt from within, was menacing the space of national identity. The "one blood with England" of Melville's prophecy can be read postcolonially as a promise of biblical father-son continuity, both rejecting the menace to unique identity, and supporting a renewed special destiny.

In the parallel with the Jeremiad, *Israel Potter* shows this new orientation of the symbolic space of nationality: if, as Bercovitch has argued, the Jeremiad is inspired by the certainty of who "we are" as Americans, constructed in the opposition between the the Egypt of the Old World and the Canaan of the New, Melville's novel instead parallels the Old World with the New World of both reader and narrator. Their apparent analogies are social injustice, revolutionary fervor, masking, ferocity, and bloodshed. Their differences, in favor of the New World, are moral virtue, resistance, fidelity. The European world parallels the exile of the promise, and in this it is identical with the American. Their difference is in value and can only be solved by a significant return of the New World messianic spirit. *White-Jacket's* biblically harmonious interpretation of the course of American destiny ended with: "national selfishness is unbounded philanthropy". Israel Potter is *no* beggar because the American collective "we" bears the riches of revolutionary moral value in the modern world: "we can not do a good to America but we give alms to the world".

In this belief the "revolutionary" analogy between Old and New World reveals its imperfection and makes the Jeremiad of *Israel Potter* a text which claims a "new identity" or a more "universal" answer to "what is an American"; by projecting Americanness on Europe's parallel ground, Melville attempts to show America's unique value: for, as his prophetic formulations suggest, America is, or will (may) yet be, for *no* other is, "the Israel of our time".

In *Our Old Home* Hawthorne mentions Israel Potter in relation to the American claimants. Old men who return to America, like Israel Potter, are bound to find there the "worst form of disappointment which comes under the guise of a long-cherished and late-accomplished purpose". In the perpetually changing American world, nothing is any longer recognizable for the returning immigrant; the very street where this expatriated Rip Van Winkle used to live "had transferred itself to New Jerusalem, and he must seek it there" (*Our Old Home*, 1970, 15). Melville's drive towards a New Jerusalem on earth is read ironically by Hawthorne; still it is read in connection to his own claim to the past, and to the emergence of a new theme, the "international theme". The invention of which links, once again, Melville to Hawthorne, and to the modern novel (Lanati, 1987, 189). The 1850s epistemological crisis is not overcome by either Melville or Hawthorne: the silence of the first, and the failure to complete his romances of the second are evidence enough. Still both Hawthorne and Melville work toward the transformation of the American dream into the project for a new universality.

Part Two

Usable Pasts and Collective Memories

America does not repel the past . . . is not so impatient as has been supposed that the slough still sticks to opinions and manners and literature while the life which served its requirements had passed into the new life of the new forms . . . [she] perceives that the corpse is slowly borne from the eating and sleeping rooms of the house . . . "

—Walt Whitman, Preface to *Leaves of Grass* (1855)

Please to remember
The Fifth of November,
Gunpowder treason and plot;
I know of no reason
Why gunpowder treason
Should ever be forgot!

—Nursery Rhyme

On the Fourth of July

Israel Potter is a fiction of history perceived as an "authentic" cultural artifact and debated as a faithful account of history. While this mixed reception points to questions about the counterposition of history as a factual or a literary discourse, what is relevant in our analysis of Melville's novel is the quality of "historicity" in a literary artifact—the "how" and the "what" it contributes to the contemporary process of figuring a national past of value, a "usable past" that necessarily is a cultural formation of historical truth.

The permanence of the past in the present, which the intertextuality of American biblical exegesis has turned into the paradigm of national value, is enforced by two historically referential signs which are crucial to the contemporary cultural debate over the national collective memory. These are the Fourth of July and the Bunker Hill Monument, respectively the date of the Declaration of Independence ritualized into a popular celebration, and a monument that fixes in stone a revolutionary beginning. Both signs presuppose the fact that the American past is culturally remembered, and has become collectively recognized, and both stand for the ambiguity of what they presently celebrate.

In the "authentic record" of the source, Israel does not return to Boston on the Fourth of July, 1826, but to New York on May 17, 1823. By choosing as a historically referential sign a popular ritual which celebrates a date in history, Melville links an anthropological concern with the concern for history. This is one of the undisputed novelties introduced in fiction by the historical novel. Rituals of festivity are in Walter Scott's novels, no less than in those of James Fenimore Cooper, mainly occasions for "scenes" which help to give the illusion of historical verisimilitude: see, for example, the Tournament in *Ivanhoe* and the Festival of the Poppinjay in *Old Mortality*, or the shooting of the pigeons in *The Pioneers* and the several Indian rites in the *Leatherstocking Novels*. Nathaniel Hawthorne's "The Maypole of Merrymount" qualifies this tradition—the Maypole was the central feature of Scott's Poppinjay—through the unification of ritual and history, by making the ritual symbolize all the historical hegemonic forces it stood against. Still, Hawthorne makes ritual symbolize history, as in "My Kinsman Major Molineaux", which fictionalizes the passage to maturity of the youth by resorting to the tar-and-feathering ritual. This rite was made historically "authentic" in pre-revolutionary practice and collectively recalled as one form of the accomplished "rite of passage" of the Revolution (Shaw, 1981).

The "Glorious Fourth", as a sign both of a future, collective memory of history and of the ritual celebrating an accomplished rite of passage, was first envisioned by John Adams. In a letter to Abigail on July 3, 1776, he wrote:

> I am apt to believe that it will be celebrated by succeeding Generations as the great anniversary Festival. It ought to be commemorated, as the Day of Deliverance, by solemn Acts of Devotion to God Almighty. It ought to be solemnized with Pomp and Parade, with Shows, Games, Sports, Guns, Bells, Bonfires and Illuminations, from one end of this continent to the other, from this Time forward forever more (Butterfield, 1975, 142).

At first a religious celebration, July Fourth became an occasion for secular frolicking and banqueting; the early thanksgiving gave way to endless Fourth-of-July addresses, carrying with them the secularization of biblical language and debated political issues. The height of Fourth-of-July celebrations was reached in 1826, when the distinctive trait of the celebratory speeches was the representation of America as the modern Israel, and of the Revolution as the providential release from the Egyptian bondage of Great Britain. It was also not unusual in the 1820s and 30s to have Revolutionary War veterans read the Declaration of Independence to the audience and complain of denied pensions (Pettus Hay, 1967, 192).

The 1826 Fourth of July memorably marked the fiftieth anniversary of the Declaration of Independence, but it was also the day both John Adams and Thomas Jefferson died: as the sign of the national "rite of passage" and a day of mourning it becomes a fitting historical symbol for Israel's return after fifty years of exile.

John McWilliams strangely maintains that the year of Israel's return was 1825, the same year of Webster's first Bunker Hill Address (McWilliams, 1984, 185); it is, instead, the year and the day in which the ritual kept its course in the unawareness of the Fathers' deaths. With the deaths of Adams and Jefferson's the fifty-year-old nation became aware of revolutionary "closure" and was torn by an impellent necessity to start anew. "[T]he revolutionary age of America" was "closed up", with their deaths, as Edward Everett acknowledges (Everett, 1836, 1, 131). The "drama was ready to be closed. It has closed", confirmed Daniel Webster, who delivered a speech in August, 1826, a eulogy for the dead Founding Fathers, haunted with a Poesque refrain—"Adams and Jefferson are no more". The setting was the national shrine, Faneuil Hall, which, for "the first time in its history was draped in mourning".

In a telling symmetry on July 4, 1826, Israel is hustled "by a rioting crowd near Faneuil Hall" celebrating Independence Day, while his own personal drama draws to its close.

John Quincy Adams, John Adams' descendant, had already become President in 1825, in a strikingly early institutionalization of the historical, generational passage. As George Forgie maintains, this quickly consummated shift proved crucial in shaping a national rhetoric dominated by the unresolved tension between fathers and sons, the party of the future and the party of the past (Forgie, 1979). John Quincy Adams himself coined what can be considered the slogan of historical acceleration, when, celebrating the Fourth of July in 1821, he had exclaimed: "A nation was born in a day", a characteristically American abridgement of the past, as recently pointed out (Kammen, 1991, 10-11).

It was on the third of July 1775 that Trumbull's Israel, hospitalized after his Bunker Hill wound, could not witness George Washington's arrival in Boston (18), and thus began to fade away into his long exile. His return on the Fourth makes that "one day" cover the fifty-one years since Bunker Hill, and since Father Washington took command.

Contemporary critics who have underlined the mercilessness of Melville's attack on Independence day, maintain, as John McWilliams typically does, that this attack reflects the 1850s disillusionment with the post-revolutionary American character. For McWilliams the writer's insistence on false Gods and Temples in *Israel Potter* links his representative men (excluding the true Western spirit, Ethan Allen), to the Fourth, since it "does not celebrate an uprising of the folk against oppressive redcoats" but dignifies "a rebellion manipulated by self-seeking leaders who use the common citizen's libertarian feelings" (McWilliams, 1984, 188). Melville's Fourth of July can be read as the sign of history's perverted ways, but also of individual resistance. As Emerson wrote in his journal in the summer of 1854:

> The American independence! that is a legend. *Your Independence*! that is the question of all the Present. Have you fought out that? & settled it once and again, & once for all in the minds of all persons with whom you have to do, that you and your sense of right, & fit & fair, are an invincible, indestructible somewhat, which is not to be bought or cajoled or frighted away? That done, & victory inscribed on your eyes and brow and voice, the other American freedom begins instantly to have some meaning & support (Emerson, 1982, 456).

The morally redeeming quality of Emerson's individualism supports a renewed sense of national "independence". There is an analogy between the Fourth of Israel's homecoming and the contemporary parallels between national independence and individual freedom, once the democratic merger between the reader and narrator of Israel's story is considered.

There is, as Vito Amoruso perceptively suggests, a deep—if conflictual—ideological, "organic", affinity between Melville and his contemporaries. Sharing with them the belief in foundational American truths, his isolation and his "attacks" are more a matter of differing intensity, than of qualitative difference (Amoruso, 1969, 77). In this perspective *Israel Potter* appears as a parallel text to the mid-century revisionist interpretations of the national past. These were revisions inspired by a post-revolutionary spirit of vindication: in this spirit, the issue became prominent as to whom, among the various self-styled descendants of the Revolutionary Fathers, the Fourth would morally belong. A revisionist historian, Richard Hildreth, could write in the "Advertisement" to a new *History of the United States of America* (1849-52)—the first two volumes of which Melville bought in 1851— "of centennial sermons and Fourth-of-July orations, whether professedly such or in the guise of history, there are more than enough", but only to cleanse the contemporary memory of the Revolutionary Fathers from the grotesque make-up that hides their true and unperishable qualities—"always earnest, downright, manly, and sincere".

Since the 1840s, blacks had refused to celebrate the Fourth, settling on the Fifth of July, often recalling biblical Egyptian bondage to describe the condition of the slaves in the United States. On the fifth of July, 1852, Frederick Douglass had delivered his famous address "What to the slave is the Fourth of July?", vindicating the Founding Father's lesson as a means of deliverance for his "exiled" race. The liberal abolitionists also claimed to be the true interpreters of Independence Day, as Charles Sumner's controversial 1845 Fourth-of-July oration in Boston testifies. America's chance to renew its revolutionary "grandeur", said Sumner, was the July Fourth legacy of democracy, peace, and justice, and not the "damnosa hereditas" of the Revolution, war and civil strife (Sumner, 1845).

Since the 1830s the revisionist spirit invested in the Fourth had stimulated the practice of rewriting the Declaration of Independence. By another meaningful coincidence, this tradition was started on July Fourth 1826, when the British social reformer Robert Owen delivered an oration entitled "Declaration of Mental Independence" in which he urged Americans to complete the "unfinished work of the Revolution" through collective social liberation. The rights of both workers and women were equally written in the same fashion, including Young America's "Declaration of Rights of the Industrial Congress" (1845) and the 1848 Women's Rights Convention's "Declaration of Sentiments and Resolution" (Foner, 1976).

Lamentably, yet consistent with women's historical struggle to become subjects of history, no woman appears in Melville's historical fictions. The women in his household, however, seem to have been concerned with their Independence. As Hennig Cohen has reported, there is a letter from Helen Briggs Melville to her sister, Augusta

Melville, written probably before *Israel Potter*'s first installment appeared in *Putnam's*, that hails its publication as follows:

> I shall be quite wild to make the acquaintance of "Israel Potter", and have the Fourth of July come. I shall have George [her husband] pro-cure me *my* Independence—namely a new novel and a paper of candy (Cohen, 1991, 293).

What Helen Briggs, probably inspired by Augusta who was copying the manuscript, expected from the new novel was a Fourth-of-July story with which to celebrate anew her own Independence day—even if through the mediation of brother and husband. Collecting the material for the novel, Melville might have had in mind a similar intention of "celebration of independence"; he pasted a newspaper account of Pittsfield's July Fourth celebrations in 1850 on his copy of Charles Dudley Field's *History of the County of Berkshire*, and in 1853, he was invited to deliver the Fourth of July oration for "fellow citizens" of the Berkshires (Cohen, 1991, 292). These may appear trivial questions since, rather than stressing the "found" quality of referents, historical narrations tend to display the production of their signs, to "constitute" them, by incorporating their referentiality (Barthes, 1981, 16-7). *Israel Potter*'s subtitle, "a Fourth-of-July Story", disappeared when it was published as a book. The subtitle itself, however, may have generated the final chapters of the novel, which Melville actually wrote while the story was running in installments. Accordingly, the reference to the Fourth of July finds an earlier tex-tual correspondence in a parallel ritual, Guy Fawkes' Day, the day of Israel Potter's arrival in London as a wretched exile: "It was late on a Monday morning, in November—a Blue Monday—a Fifth of November—Guy Fawkes' Day!" (158).

In 1849, Melville set foot on English soil on the fifth of November, and in his journal he records the event with a curious historical asso-ciation: "Some centuries ago a person called Julius Caesar jumped ashore about in this place, & took possession. It was Guy Fawke's [sic] Day also" (Melville, 1948, 21). This was Melville's return to England after his first voyage there as a sailor on the *St. Lawrence*, which anchored off Liverpool on July Fourth, 1839.

"Guy Fawkes' Day" was the popular reenactment of a liberation; its ritual centered on burning an effigy of a seventeenth-century Papist conspirator. The effigy, clothed in grotesque garments, was usually accompanied by other similar, lesser figures called, by extension, Guys. (This is the OED etymology for our democratic *guy*). Children would ask for money to buy the fireworks after the burning, crying the begging formula "A penny for the Old Guy".

Sustained by the textual parallelism between England and America, a symmetry is suggested between the English and American popular festivals of liberation. In fact, Guy Fawkes' Day, or Pope's Day, was celebrated in New England since its early days (Hall, 1989, 210-11). Similar celebrations continued into the pre-revolutionary era and took on such an unexpected irreverence that the Colonial government came to consider them as dangerous expressions of popular rebellion. The children who accompanied the effigy were pre-revolutionary youths promising figurative fireworks for the Colonial power. Their ritual reenactment took on a historical meaning similar to the tar-and-feathering of Hawthorne's "rite of passage" (Shaw, 1981). In "Alice Doane's Appeal" Hawthorne muses on Salem's Fifths of November, which were apparently celebrated till 1817. After 1817, Pope's Day's purifying fire was transferred to Fourth of July eve (Robotti, 1948, 37). Hawthorne writes:

> We are a people of the present and have no heartfelt interest in olden time. Every fifth of November, in commemoration of they know not what, or rather without an idea beyond the momentary blaze, the young men scare the town with bonfires on this haunted height [Gallows Hill], but never dream of paying funeral honors to those who died so wrongfully, and without a coffin or a prayer, were buried here (Hawthorne, 1982, 206).

The meaning of Pope's Day is apparently forgotten, emptied out by the excitement of a "momentary blaze".

Israel's Guy Fawkes' Day marks the passage from his being a "slave" in a brick kiln—whose fire does not purify but envelopes him, like a brick, in "the dull smoke" of the "torments" of billions—to becoming an unbeggarly "poor player" who "succeeds better in life's tragedy than comedy". His London-City of Dis is buried under cold funereal images, resonating with Faneuil Hall draped in mourning:

> Hung in long, sepulchral arches of stone, the black, besmoked bridge seemed a huge scarf of crape, festooning the river across . . . Meantime, here and there, like awaiting hearses, the coal-scows drifted along, poled, broadside, pell mell to the current (159).

Israel's return on the Fourth is anticipated both by factual detail— Israel being "wedged in" among the crowd—and by poetic parallels that stress the infernal rather than purgatorial nature of his passage.

Still, in a crowd of "uninvoked ghosts in Hades", Potter acquires the spirit of prophecy: "Israel's heart was prophetically heavy; foreknowing that being of this race, felicity could never be its lot". The blind youth can now become the old man with foresight, who nonetheless is a parallel to "blind" tragic heroes: "a plebeian Lear or Oedipus" (165).

Through the parallel of sightlessness between Israel and classic tragic heroes, Oedipus to Lear, the text suggests the possibility of a tragic ending for *Israel Potter*. As Georg Lukács has maintained, in tragedies the dualistic forces of man and Gods either exclude history, or transform it: "God must leave the stage, but must yet remain a spectator; that is the historical possibility of tragic epochs"; historical tragedy is a paradox:

> the metaphysical paradox of the relationship between tragic man and historical existence; the paradox of inner distance between the spectator and the characters, the paradox between the characters' different degrees of life and life intensity, the clash between the symbolic and the lifelike in the characters and events of historical drama (Lukács, 1981, 90-1).

The paradoxical unrealization of historical tragedy is buried in Israel's sight: as a type, he is blind when history dooms him as a force of Fate, but as a tragic character, he "sees" when he is in the passage out of it, in the symbolic time-in-between Guy Fawkes and the Fourth of July.

The return of sight makes the reader's identification with the character possible and, at the same time, marks the distance between the character's personal fate and the moral vision of the spectator. Back in history on the Fourth of July 1826, Israel does not die when run over by the festive crowds; he escapes the carnivalesque parade of the Fourth of July of his unrecognized homecoming, and reads "the gilt letters" inscribed on a "broidered banner":

"BUNKER-HILL.
1775.
GLORY TO THE HEROES THAT FOUGHT!" (167)

The letters are not of real gold, as they should be in a tragedy. They are satirically "gilt letters" that the reader may recognize as a false celebration of history. Israel may become a moral hero, truer to history than its celebrations. By both contrast and homology, his true-to-history character receives the "poetic justice" of the same eulogy lavished upon Jefferson and Adams. When in the last chapter of the novel, entitled "Requiescat in pace", the Fourth-of-July representation gives way to the eulogy, Israel's type becomes a "Type of forever arrested intentions, and a long life still rotting in mishap". It is the mishap of the "exile" *still* in the present, that coexists with the persistence of "*our*": the communal moral ownership of history of "we" the descendants.

Israel Potter's readers are presented the possibility of reading the text as a reenactment of an Independence ritual, both a burning of the "conspirator" and an accomplished act of insubordination vindicating the people's rights, as suggested by the combined traits of Guy Fawkes and Fourth of July. For these readers *Israel Potter*'s "usable past" is to be found in the permanence of an individual reenactment of national foundation. Melville's version of the "usable past" can be interpreted by stressing its metaphysical aspect; the cultural type of such an aspect however, a ritual, becomes "verisimilar" to the reader's understanding by the intersection of history and anthropology. In this, *Israel Potter* takes its place in the tradition of the Moderns. "A penny for the Old Guy", the subtitle of T.S. Eliot's "The Hollow

Men" (1925), sounds like the invitation accepted by Melville's future reader. In the opening lines of Eliot's poem, effigies stuffed like scarecrows wait for the consuming fire. The speaking voice is one of them, and he is the sightless persona descending to "death's dream kingdom". Eliot's reference to the commemoration of the fifth of November "reflects the custom of burning in effigy the bearer of local guilt"; in accordance with the *The Golden Bough*'s interpretation, the straw man is the scapegoat whose burning rids "his folk of accumulated ill-chance" (Smith, 1956, 105). It seems worth noticing that at the moment of Melville's revival—*Israel Potter* was published again, after more than sixty years, in 1922—a modernist poem paralleled the Guy Fawkes' symbolism within the novel. There is another possible link between Melville's novel and Eliot's poem. "The Hollow Men"'s famous line: "Paralysed force, gesture without motion", is expanded into:

> Between the idea
> And the reality
> Between the motion
> And the act
> Falls the Shadow
>
> *For thine is the Kingdom* (Eliot, 1963, 89-2).

Eliot here rewrites Brutus's speech in Shakespeare's *Julius Caesar* (II.1), a passage Melville underlined (Cowen, 1987, 2, 432). Melville's own "one day" of independence may be seen as the "shadow" cast in history, the space in between idea and reality, and motion and act. In Eliot's modern notion, history is told as gaps to be gauged in cultural signs which represent the tradition of the past. The interpreters' ritual reenactments may make them significant again. Twentieth-century anthropology is, after all, what allows Eliot to universalize history anew and support its conversion into Christian metaphysics.

ON THE BUNKER HILL MONUMENT

When *Israel Potter* appeared as a book in 1855, Melville dropped the subtitle and added a one-page dedication: "To His Highness the Bunker Hill Monument", dated on the anniversary date of the battle, June 17, 1854. Melville's shift from the symbolism of the Fourth of July to that of Bunker Hill may be seen as a vindication of the spirit of '75; this spirit was the popular embodiment of the historiographical interpretation of the Revolution as the event which realized the original, democratic impulse of the Puritan Fathers, as opposed to or contained in celebrating the actual Revolutionary Fathers. In the tradition of dedications, however, Melville offers *Israel Potter* to an excellent patron, but also to a fellow spirit and competitor, to the monument as a conspicuous sign of American historical discourse. *Pierre*'s dedication to Mount Greylock sounded like a dedication to the Majesty of American nature; *Israel Potter*'s instead evokes the Highness of American History, the capitalized sign of its discourses. Through the logic of parallel and difference, the Fourth of July ritualizes in history the advent of a liberated new era, while the monument fixes, in the stone of rhetoric, its collective memory.

The dedication has received modern critical attention because of its ironic tone, and its attack on hollow or false celebrations of history. It is indeed presented by Melville himself as the catalyst of a critical discourse, by satirically making the Monument the Official Reader, prominent because it is the Official Speaker of the rewriting of national history. Melville's ironic or even sarcastic attitude here was noted by only one of his early reviewers: "A tinge of obscure sarcasm pervades the book, most apparent in its dedication to the Bunker Hill Monument" (*National Magazine*, 6, 1855, 340-1). This accusation stands out in *Israel Potter*'s contemporary reception which almost unanimously praises the novel's Americanism, or, as the anonymous reviewer in the *Commercial Advertiser* put it, Melville's work is thoroughly "saturated with American sentiment" (22 March, 1855). There is, however, an undoubtedly disrespectful tone in the dedication, the targets of which are both the Monument, and the writings of history, including the "artistic" ones. "General fidelity" is the centerpiece of Melville's sarcasm:

> Well aware that in your Highness's eye the merit of the story must be in the general fidelity to the main drift of the original narrative, I forbore in any way to mitigate the hard fortunes of my hero; and particularly towards the end, though sorely tempted, durst not substitute for the allotment of Providence any artistic recompense of poetical justice, so that no one can complain of the doom of my closing chapters more profoundly than myself (viii).

"General fidelity" to history is the claim of both monument and novel: in his Highness's eyes, it means the granitic correspondence between historical events and celebratory discourse; for the writer as the editor of a historical source, it means that poetic justice "strongly" demands an atonement for Israel's story, that might contradict His Highness' emphatic correspondences.

Both novel and monument are signs of a collective memory of the past. Their language is different; yet stones and words may show their interchangeability and their difference within a common cultural discourse of the past. This may account for the competition between novel and monument, as to which better represents or even celebrates national memory; the dedication also suggests that the novel aims at incorporating the sign of the Monument within its own system of language, as part of the novel's symbolic configuration.

The Bunker Hill Monument was an expression of the 1820s fervor of revolutionary celebration. Monumentality as a token of respect for the dead was suggested by the debate over the conservation of Washington's residence and tomb, and in 1824—the year Trumbull's *Life* was published—zealous Boston citizens started a widely publicized subscription which allowed construction to begin a year later. It was to be (and is) a daringly tall obelisk of New England granite. Appropriately the first stone was laid in the presence of the Marquis Lafayette, and a son of New England, Daniel Webster, delivered the address; he gave a second speech when the monument was complete, in 1843. Over the twenty years it took to build, through several disruptions its progress was constantly and apprehensively watched not only by Boston's most prominent citizens, but by the whole country (Frothingham, 1896).

In 1846, George Edward Ellis's *Sketches of Bunker Hill Battle and Monument* (1843) was presented to Melville. It contains a rationale of the meaning of the monument itself as a "tribute of respect to the patriots who, in an early day of the Revolution, risked all that was dear to them as individuals, on a fearful hazard for the good of their common country." It also suggests that a yearning for recognition, for becoming part of the collective memory of history might have sustained those early heroes: some of their "fortitude", he writes, might have been "borrowed from the conviction that their country would honor their memory, and that their children would mark the spot where they suffered". The actual monument is the evidence that they have become part of the nation's collective memory, but also, significantly, Ellis defines the revolutionary ideals of the Fathers within their desire for celebration. For Ellis, the time of celebration marks the prosperous present of the nation, and from this standpoint he, like Webster in 1843, urges his countrymen to forget animosities against the Old Country, in order to realize the promise of America as universal exemplum.

"All that we desire to commemorate by this towering pile now reared on the battlefield is patriotism and self-sacrifice", Ellis maintains, before describing the actual battle. As a playful instance of feelings at the eve of the Revolutionary War, a handbill containing an Address to the British soldiers after Washington had cut off their provisions is reproduced:

Prospect Hill	Bunker Hill
[the Insurgents' post]	[the British post]
I Seven dollars a month	I Threepence a day
II Fresh Provisions and in plenty	II Rotten Salt Pork
III Health	III The Scurvy
IV Freedom, ease, affluence and a good farm. (Ellis, 1843, 161)	IV Slavery, Beggary and want.

It is a fair assumption that Melville might have seen the irony in Ellis's reversals between celebration and the value of historical memory, and between American native "poverty and liberty" and the false riches of propaganda. As to the "towering pile", Melville's handwritten annotation in David Dudley Field's *A History of the County of Berkshire* (1829) reads: "old man—soldier minute man", seemingly a comment both on the mention of the many unknown and uncelebrated soldiers from the region who "sacrificed their lives in the cause of the country". This annotation resonates with the following passage, describing the Berkshires landscape, underlined by the writer:

> The most remarkable mountain in the town [Stockbridge] is Monument Mountain . . . It derived its name from a rude monument of stones . . . The Pile was 6 or 7 feet in diameter, circular at its base, and raised in the form of an obtuse cone . . . over the grave of one of the Aborigines . . . Every Indian who passed the place threw a stone upon the tomb of his countrymen. By this slow method of accumulation the heap rose in a long series of years to the size just mentioned . . . The same mode of raising monuments for the dead . . . except in one particular, had existed among other nations. The Israelites raised a similar monument for Achan, for the king of Ai, and for Absalom. Whether this was done from motives of general respect for the dead and thus in conformity to a general custom, or with a design to express their abhorrence of the persons buried, will admit of a doubt. The manner in which the phrase "the stones of the pit" is used by the Prophet Isaiah, (xiv; 19), an allusion, I presume, to the same practice, does not remove the uncertainty (Field, 1829, 224).

As has been noticed, stone-symbols are a conspicuous feature of *Israel Potter*. The historical irony of the granite Bunker Hill monument's celebrative intentions and its slow construction finds its echo in Field's doubt as to its its meaning, whether it means "general respect", or "general fidelity", or "abhorrence" for the dead. Field suggests an ambiguous solution to such an uncertain meaning by characteristically coupling the Indians with the Israelites and resorting to the evidence of the Bible, to Isaiah, the prophet of the Babylonian captivity but also of Israel's exile. The passage referred to reads as follows:

But thou art cast out of thy grave like an abominable branch, *and as* the raiment of those that are slain, thrust through with a sword, that go down to the stones of the pit; as a carcasse trodden under feet (Isaiah, 14:19).

Israel Potter, His Fifty Years of Exile, which opens with a Berkshire description of stony walls, begins the final transition to the same landscape, when Israel looks towards the battlefield:

> It was on Copp's Hill, within the city bounds, one of the enemy's positions during the fight, that our wanderer found his best repose that day. Sitting here on a mound in the graveyard, he looked off across Charles River towards the battle ground, whose incipient monument at that period was hard to see, as a struggling sprig of corn in a chilly spring (167).

From Copp's Hill, where the "potter's field" graveyard of biblical and historical memory is located, the "incipient monument" is compared to "a struggling sprig of corn in a chilly winter". An image of promising yet imperilled nature is substituted for the monument's stone basement.

In the London fog of Guy Fawkes' Day, Israel had similarly rested at the foot of Nelson's column in Trafalgar Square, its torch, a denied biblical beacon of light: "no Pillar of fire by the night, except the cold column of the monument: two hundred feet beneath the mocking gilt flames on whose top, at the stone base, the shiverer, of midnight often laid down" (161). In fact Nelson's monument was completed only a few months before Melville's arrival in London, and its erection started in 1843, a long time after Israel's return to America.

"The torch of liberty", Edward Everett told the veterans in his audience in Concord on April 19, 1825, is to be passed "in all the splendor of its kindling, bright and flaming, to those who stand next in the line". This is all the more urgent as the venerable revolutionary survivors are "dropping round us like the leaves of autumn" (Everett, 1836, 78). Biblical "heaps of stones", "carcasses thrown under feet", "abominable branches" resonate with bright "Pillars of fire" and a poetic "struggling sprig of corn", and effect the transition from the sarcasm surrounding the monument's realized celebration to its incipient poetic image.

Contemporary readers are the addressees of this "rite of passage", since theirs is the memory of the granite monument. This is a memory to which Daniel Webster gave words. In his story "The Stone Face" (1850), Hawthorne had mildly satirized Webster as the aspiring, wise "Man of Prophecy" who failed to actually become so because his features could not be recognized in the New England granite of Mount Greylock Stone Face, a true work of American Nature. Similarly Henry David Thoreau ends *Walden*—published in August, 1854, while *Israel Potter* was running in installments—by reformulating his attack against contemporary degeneration, opposing his own celebration of nature to other hollow celebrations: "What are men celebrating? They are all on a committee of arrangements, and hourly expect a speech from somebody. God is only the president of the day, and Webster is his orator" (Thoreau, 1970, 445).

William Dillingham has argued that Webster's Bunker Hill Addresses of 1825 and 1843 inspired Melville's own dedication to the monument; Daniel Webster has also been seen as the figure standing behind Moby Dick's "Pyramidal silence", since he had often been associated with a Pyramid by his enthusiastic contemporaries, and because of his highly acclaimed rhetorical trick in the second Bunker Hill Address (Dillingham, 1986, 254; Heimert, 1963). Referring to the monument, Webster had said:

> I have spoken of the loftiness of its purpose . . . That well-known purpose it is which causes us to look up to it with a feeling of awe. It is itself the orator of this occasion. It is not from my lips, it could not be from any human lips, that the strain of eloquence is this day to flow most competent, to move and excite the vast multitudes around me. The powerful speaker stands motionless before us (Webster, 1895, 32).

Here the orator paused with his outstretched arm, pointing at the monument in order to let everybody hear its meaningful silent utterance. Then resuming, he interpreted it as follows:

To-day it speaks to us. Its future auditories will be the successive generations of man as they rise up before it and gather around it. Its
speech will be of patriotism and courage; of civil and religious liberty;
of free government; of the moral improvement and elevation of mankind; and of the immortal memory of those who, with heroic devotion,
have sacrificed their lives for their country (33).

Webster gives voice to the silent "powerful speaker", thus becoming
himself the monument of national memory, and, possibly, Melville's
"Great Biographer":

. . . seeing that your Highness . . . may, in the loftiest sense, be
deemed the Great Biographer: the national commemorator of such of
the anonymous privates of June 17, 1775, who may never have received
other requital than the solid reward of your granite (viii).

There is also another Webster's address speaking for the Monument as
the Great Biographer and the great orator as its exchangeable human
form. In 1832, Webster had addressed the national Republican Convention on behalf of Melville's paternal grandfather who, at the age of
78, was removed as Naval Officer for the Port of Boston by the new
administration of Andrew Jackson. Melville's dedication is inscribed
on the senventy-eighth anniversary of the Declaration of Independence; as Michael Rogin has shown, both of Melville's grandfathers,
two Revolutionary heroes, played an important part in Melville's own
visions of challenge and defeat (Rogin, 1983). While Grandfather
Gansevoort was a member of the revolutionary "knightly" order of the
Cincinnati—a form of the American aristocracy discussed in *Pierre*'s
first chapter—Major Thomas Melville is recorded by none other than
Oliver Wendell Holmes in his poem "The Last Leaf" (1831-2), as a
dejected old man walking the streets of Boston leaning on a cane, dis-
playing both "the monumental pomp" of a forgotten glorious age and
an aspect *"so forlorn"*. "And he shakes his feeble head,/ That it seems
as if he said,/ 'They are gone' " (Holmes, 1975, 4).

Holmes says of these lines: "among the crowd of a latter generation
he reminded me of a withered leaf which has held its stem through
the storms of autumn and winter". In Webster's address on Thomas
Melville's behalf—published in 1851 in the first volume of his *Works*,

where it follows the Bunker Hill speeches—the old man is buried in a rhetoric of generalization:

> If a man holding an office necessary for his daily support had presented himself covered with the scars of wounds received in every battle, from Bunker Hill to Yorktown, these would not have protected him from this rackless rapacity . . . He was a personification of the spirit of 1776, one of the earliest to venture in the cause of liberty . . . His character, his standing, his Revolutionary services, were all well known; but they were known to no purpose . . . (Webster, 1851, I, 260).

Webster's rhetoric was no help for Thomas Melville, who died that same year, without rehabilitation. His scars, like Israel's, "proved his only medals". Yet the "rackless rapacity" that Webster attributes to the Jackson Administration, reversing the accusation of theft which had been levelled against the old man, invokes the final biblical resonance with the monument. As Field's *A History of the County of Berkshire* suggests: "The Israelites raised a similar monument for Achan, for the king of Ai, and for Absalom". Accused either of theft or bribe and rapacity, both Achan and Absalom die in disgrace, and while the first, with his whole family, is stoned to death and consumed by fire, the second, entangled in tree-branches, is defenselessly killed, cast into the pit and covered by the heap of stones.

In his lifetime, Absalom "had taken and reared for himself a pillar which *is* in the king's dale: for he said, I have no son to keep my name in remembrance" (Sam., 18: 18). At the very end of *Israel Potter*, some "sunken stone" in a Berkshire field is suddenly hit by a laborer's plough. Israel recognizes the family hearthstone, buried in nature. He is thus connected back to his father, his past, and his country. In Israel's "resurrection" in the Berkshires—"The exile's presence in these old mountain townships proved less a return than a resurrection" (168)—the stone relic matches the "struggling sprig of corn" of the incipient monument: they are both poetic "humble" signs of a renewed historical memory, to be contrasted with "towering piles" because of their superior "fidelity" to the American experience, democratic because organic to the soil.

AN OLD TOMBSTONE RETOUCHED

B rian Rosenberg has read *Israel Potter* as a disagreement with Carlyle's "Heroic in History", and there is undoubtedly a critique of hero-worship in the monument as the Great Biographer and in the novel's representative men (Rosenberg, 1987). In the dedication, Melville refers to the Harvard historian Jared Sparks, whose works do not mention such humble soldiers as Israel Potter: "That the name here noted should not have appeared . . . may or may not be a matter for astonishment" (viii). The target of Melville's irony is apparently academic historiography. Sparks, the editor of the *Library of American Biography*, monumentalized as gentlemen and heroes, in twelve and ten volumes respectively, George Washington and Benjamin Franklin. Melville probably used Sparks' Franklin volumes for his portrait of the old Sage and convincingly shatters the historian's own idea of writing American history as the biography of its great men.

Still Melville shares Carlyle's and Emerson's concern with "biography" as the viable form of a discourse of history. In Rosenberg's post-modern reading, Melville's novel appears, instead, as a radical attack on any form of historical writing. Since the writings of the past cannot be reliably read, Rosenberg argues, the inspired artist is forced to distill some "ahistorical meaning that applies with special force to the past and the future" (Rosenberg, 1987, 177). *Israel Potter* may be an excellent example for readers of "indeterminacy", yet its discourse is one of a "usable past" paralleling contemporary discourses, and, in the logic of parallelism, revealing analogy, not identity or separation. The solution of "ahistorical meaning" configured in the novel is in itself part of the cultural construction of the past shared by Melville and his contemporaries; and as shown by the configuration of biblical exegesis, it is through the experience of its "historicity" that the sacred becomes historical again. Rewriting an "authentic" autobiography from the past, Melville transforms it into a national biography whose protagonist is an American native type. Still Potter is a reliable type of history, and his function is to elicit a reader's response to American history in the making, as shown by the historical content of Melville's prophecies.

One could say that, by the 1850s, telling history in fictional form requires the writing in the text of a notion of the past which, as any notion, is ahistorical, but which is, at the same time, a new or renewed paradigm of an American discourse of history. This discourse claims its "authenticity" in the intersection of the "representational" and the "symbolic". And, as in Melville's *Israel Potter*, symbols are signs that parallel sources of history to their interpretation.

By another of those symmetries which abound in any literary *oeuvre* and are particularly relevant in Melville's—in which echoes from his own previous works often stand side by side with echoes or quotations from other texts—the Messiah passage in *White-Jacket* follows a quotation from an 1824 *Edinborough Review's* article on flogging. Trumbull's 1824 *Life* is presented in the dedication as an obsolete pamphlet, and with the same purposeful irony Melville introduces his quote from the Scottish magazine. Though flogging is the legacy of the past still active in the present, *White-Jacket's* narrator gives voice to a transcendental creed:

> The world has arrived at a period which renders it the part of Wisdom to pay homage to the prospective precedents of the Future in preference to those of the Past. The past is dead, and has no resurrection; but the Future is endowed with such a life that it lives to us even in anticipation. The Past is in many things the foe of mankind; the Future is in all things, our friend. In the past is no hope; the future is both hope and fruition. The past is the textbook of tyrants; the Future the Bible of the Free. Those who are solely governed by the Past stand like Lot's wife, crystallized in the act of looking backward, and forever incapable of looking before (Melville, 1984, 505).

"The prospective precedents of the Future" are by Emersonian definition, the "usable past". For Melville, however, such precedents do not exclude that flogging is a historical fact recorded by an authoritative source and still practiced in the present of the story. The dedication of *Israel Potter* pushes further the relation between history as a reliable account of the past, that cannot be suppressed, and the notion of a usable past. *White Jacket*'s reference to Lot's wife, "crystallized in the act of looking backward, and forever incapable of looking before", is replaced by a reference to the New Testament: Israel Potter's "blurred record", "like the crutch-marks of the cripple by the Beautiful Gate" of Jerusalem (Acts, 3: 1-11), has gone "out of print". The irony is that no crutch-marks are left behind by the lame man healed by Peter (Cohen, 1991, 349). Israel's limp, instead, leaves its historical mark at the gate of the nation in Melville's novel.

The notion of the usable past cannot be formulated without the awareness of a collective historical memory; the use is determined by an idea of future that orients the selection of memories. Melville's belief in the continuity of American history, though dramatically or even tragically asserted, sustains his representation of Israel Potter's story. As his version of the great men of the past and of the Bunker Hill Monument shows, the target of his satire is faulty recognition, and false or repressed memory of history. The abridgment of disturbing events from national memory is immoral, and it is so because of the moral vision that has inspired American history since its beginning. To look backward in *Israel Potter* means to read the past in a disturbing, but not unreliable, historical document and at the same time to assess the morality of national historical memory.

Both Hawthorne and Melville wrote historical fictions of the national past. Both, in different ways, are concerned with "half-buried" or "blurred" images or accounts that leave their traces on the present. Disturbing though these traces are within optimistic projections into the future, still they have to be included in narrations of the past to prove the morality of historical continuity. For both writers, the notion of a usable past shuns forgetfulness, and, at the cost of the age's "optative mood", their fictions "remember". Intellectuals as different as George Santayana and Sigmund Freud thus formulated the modern notion of the past:

> Those who cannot rememember the past are condemned to repeat it (Santayana, 1905, 1, 284).

[The individual is] obliged to *repeat* the repressed material as a contemporary experience instead of . . . remembering it as something
belonging to the past (Freud, 1974, 18, 180).

Hawthorne was haunted by the possible repetition of a sinful past, as
much as Melville's Israel is condemned to repeat his past of imprisonment. The solution for this modern awareness of the return of an
upsetting past, lies, for both Santayana and Freud, in "remembering",
since remembering both frees individuals and connects them to the
past, and, both for Freud and Santayana, makes them functioning
subjects of history.

While in Hawthorne's unfinished romances "remembering" is a
narrative process, in Melville's *Israel Potter* it is the theme of the
dedication to the Monument of national memory. This theme is
expressed by ironic counterpositions: false versus true memory, partial-
ity versus comprehensiveness. And since *Israel Potter* is a historical
novel—by the minimal definition that it is set in the past and represents historical characters and events—the theme of remembering is
metanarratively linked to the tradition of written memory represented
by the historical novel.

Melville's work of resurrection of Trumbull's *Life* is presented as
"something in the light of a dilapidated old tombstone retouched"
and the reference is textualized in the last chapter's title: *Requiescat in
pace*. The "old tombstone retouched" is a topos for the "poetics" of
historical fiction. The Cameronian tombstones in Walter Scott's *Old
Mortality* may serve as its most illustrious example. The introduction
to the novel is in fact the introduction to a character of the past, Old
Mortality. He is a forgotten, poor, and aged patriot turned by
historical events, like Melville's Israel, into a wanderer. Scott summarizes his destiny as follows:

In the language of the Scripture, he left his house, his home, and his
kindred, and wandered about until the day of his death, a period of
nearly thirty years (Scott, 1895, 9).

Old Mortality, a dead man when the narration begins, is left with not
even "a small monument to his memory", though he himself in the

last years of his life toured churchyards making sure that the words covered by moss on the tombs of the Covenanters would be kept legible,

> renewing to the eyes of posterity the decaying emblems of the zeal and suffering of their forefathers, and thereby trimming, as it were, the beaconlight, which was to warn future generations to defend their religion even unto blood (9-10).

In *Old Mortality*'s tradition, *Israel Potter* performs a memorial rite for the dead, thus restoring a "beacon of light" to future generations. The "parable" of *Old Mortality* introduces a fiction of history inspired by the principle of renewing the past by representing it as it was, and as it still is, though dilapidated and covered with moss. Melville's "dilapitated old tombstone retouched" suggests a similar intent, and a difference: his narration of history does not pretend to be an eye-witness account, but bears witness through the very words of the past. Retouching the tombs of the past means to "read" the obliterated words inscribed on them anew, for the future.

As has often been noticed there is a resonance between the opening sentence of Emerson's *Nature*—"Our age is retrospective. It builds the sepulchres of the fathers" (Emerson, 1982, 7)—and Webster's second Bunker Hill speech—"We are among the sepulchres of our fathers" (Webster, 1895, 2). The two sentences differ in meaning: one suggests a new relation with the past and its books, the other a celebrated realization of the heritage of the past. Melville's own "dilapitated old tombstone retouched" marks a similar difference from the "old tombstones" of classical historical novels. The work of historical memory begun by Scott's fiction is continued, and retouched by a generational and national awareness of difference: the use to which the past is put, is the past itself.

FINAL REMARKS:
IF ALL OF HISTORY IS IN ONE MAN . . .

"If the whole of history is in one man, it is all to be explained from individual experience" (Emerson, 1983, 237). Thus Emerson in "History" summarizes the relation between the past and the doctrine of individualism. Both Hawthorne's and Melville's fictions of the past show an ideological agreement with Emerson's "new piety", that of the all-comprehensive self, able to see the past. Being the "property" of the individual, this past is projected into a future of untrammmelled potentialities in Emerson's view. Hawthorne and Melville lacked Emerson's confidence in "realized ideals"; both, however, represent the spirit of the age in their own methods of writing about the past.

> We must in ourselves see the necessary reason for every fact,—see how it could and it must be. So stand before every public and private work; before an oration of Burke, before a victory of Napoleon, before a martyrdom of Sir Thomas More, of Sidney, of Marmaduke Robinson, before a French Reign of Terror, and a Salem hanging of witches, before a fanatic Revival, and the Animal Magnetism in Paris, or in Providence. We assume that we under like influence should be alike affected, and should achieve the like; and we aim to master intellectually the steps, and reach the same height or the same degeneration, that our fellow, our proxy, has done. (Emerson, 1983, 241)

Whether by exploring the belief that "magic and all that is ascribed to it, is a deep presentiment of the powers of science", or the belief that listening to the "voice of the prophet out of the deeps of antiquity", the new man "pierces to the truth through all the confusion of tradition and the caricature of institutions" (Emerson, 1983, 253; 249), Hawthorne and Melville privilege the "first person singular" as both the receiver and shaper of a discourse of the past. Their narrative strategy is characterized by a renewed prominence of the reader's role. In the new pact that links together narrator and reader, one is the "fellow" or the "proxy" of the other. In their dialogic exchange, the personal pronouns "I" and "you", "I" and "they" tend to merge into a beholding "we" who can "see" or "read" it all. Indeed fiction becomes a substitute for reality, or history, either in the analogy between reality and produced effects of reality, or in that between authentic facts of history and their rhetoric.

The only reality the past can ever achieve is the response of the individual to its fictions. In this, Emerson showed the way, and Hawthorne and Melville paved it into their narratives. Their texts described as "symbolic" or "open-ended"—shunning "closure"— partake of the modern quality of inducing the desire of "continuity", of "inclusiveness" in their readers. Both continuity of "process", and inclusiveness in the coexistence of either sundry effects, or opposites in endless parallels point to an enlarged notion of the adressee as an ideal subjectivity which is capable to comprehend a new totality of vision. Before modernism became a literary tradition, both Melville and Hawthorne invented its fictional archetypes, by reformulating the reader's role, by showing the palimpsestic nature of any discourse, by assessing the "authenticity" of the literary artifact in its being autonomous from reality, without renouncing its "claim" to represent the world.

In fact, as Emerson says of the self confronted with history, Melville's and Hawthorne's texts stand before the past and confront it not by reproducing identical shapes, but aiming "to master intellectually the steps". Individually "reading" or "seeing anew" the past— and not "showing" the events of the past—is an exercise through which the morality of one's own history is tested. Both Hawthorne and Melville do not merely condemn or celebrate historical facts; they aim at constructing a contemporary subject of moral value who can form his own judgement of the past.

If morality is the all-American trait of individualism, when Hawthorne and Melville write about the past, they are writing about the American individual faced with the morality of history. The "morality" of their texts rests on a new "literary ethics", the ethics of individualism, which, in its higher form, sets the reader as the active, morally judgemental, protagonist of the fictive—and of the real— universe.

Moral histories in the modern era share a concern with nationalism, the more so when wars of independence are envisioned as foundational events. In this, the American experience started a tradition. In the 1850s, while new nations were claiming their independence, the American revolutionary myth of origin was being tested. The morality of the American national experience seemed both confirmed and doubted in the decade when Melville and Hawthorne wrote their stories of American claims to the past. Their obvious differences notwithstanding, both Hawthorne's unfinished romances and Melville's *Israel Potter* stage the drama of an American self who tests traditions in the effort to prove national uniqueness. And even to prove that this uniqueness both separates "us" from "them" in the name of national boundaries, and unites "us" and "them", the New and the Old World, or the past and the present, in the name of the man from the modern world, the American.

"The riddle of the age has for each a private solution", Emerson wrote in 1860 (Emerson, 1983, 943). Private solutions become the cultural trait of the age; in its panorama, they end up mattering more than riddles, since subjectivity is the notion that is to dominate the future, either in the self-reflexivity of historical—or political— discourse, or in the centrality of psychic functionings in shaping new world visions. If all history is in one man, then telling history as if it were a function of one man's eyes or of a one man's books is to make a modern, "realistic" claim to it. In their fictions of the past both Melville and Hawthorne strove to make this claim legitimate.

WORKS CITED

Abrams, M.H.   1971   *Natural Supernaturalism*, New York, Norton

Amoruso, Vito   1969   "Un mare senza rive: Melville e l'arte (II)", *Studi Americani*, 15, 75-129

Anderson, Benedict   1983   *Imagined Communities*, London, Verso

Anderson, Stuart   1981   *Race and Rapprochement*, Rutherford, Fairleigh Dickinson U.P.

Arvin, Newton   1950   *Herman Melville*, The American Men of Letters Series, William Sloane

Armstrong, Nancy   1987   *Desire and Domestic Fiction, A Political History of the Novel*, New York, Oxford U.P.

Baudelaire, Charles   1976   *Un mangeur d'opium*, Études Baudelairiennes VI-VII, Neuchâtel, Éditions de la Baconnière

Baym, Nina   1976   *The Shape of Hawthorne's Career*, Ithaca, Cornell U.P.

Barthes, Roland   1981   "The Discourse of History" in *Comparative Criticism: A Yearbook*, 3, Cambridge, Cambridge U.P., 7-18

Becker, John E.   1971   *Hawthorne's Historical Allegory: An Examination of the American Conscience*, New York, Kennikat Press

Bell, Millicent   1991   *Meaning in Henry James*, Cambridge, Harvard U.P.

Benjamin, Walter   1982   "Paris, Capital du XIXème siècle", *Das Passagen-Werk*, 1, Frankfurt, Suhrkamp

       1969   *Illuminations*, ed. by H. Arendt, New York, Schocken

Bercaw, Mary K.   1987   *Melville's Sources*, Evanston, Northwestern U.P.

Bercovitch, Sacvan   1975   *The Puritan Origins of the American Self*, New Haven , Yale U.P.

       1976   "How the Puritans Won the American Revolution", *Massachusetts Review*, 17, 597-630

       1978   *The American Jeremiad*, Madison, The University of Wisconsin Press

       1991   *The Office of the Scarlet Letter*, Baltimore, The Johns Hopkins U.P.

Berlant, Lauren   1991   *The Anatomy of National Fantasy*, Chicago, The University of Chicago Press

Berthoff, Warner   1962   *The Example of Melville*, Princeton, Princeton U.P.

Bezanson Walter E.   1982   "Historical Note", *Israel Potter*, Chicago, Northwestern U.P., 173-236

Bianchi, Ruggero	1990	"Ancora una volta, con sentimento", *Pierre o le ambiguità, Israel Potter*, 5, Milano, Mursia, lv-lxvi
Brewster, David	1843	*Letters on Natural Magic*, New York, Harper
Brodhead, Richard H.	1986	*The School of Hawthorne*, New York, Oxford U.P.
Brooke-Rose, Christine	1991	*Stories, Theories and Things*, Cambridge, Cambridge U.P.
Brumm, Ursula	1970	*American Thought and Religious Typology*, New Brunswick, Rutgers U.P.
Bush, Clive	1977	*The Dream of Reason*, New York, St. Martin Press
Butterfield, L.H. et al.	1975	*The Book of Abigail and John: Selected Letters of the Adams Family, 1762-1784*, Cambridge, Harvard U.P.
Cabibbo, Paola (ed.)	1983	*Melvilliana*, Roma, Bulzoni
Cagidemetrio, Alide	1989	"A Plea for Fictional Histories and Old Time 'Jewesses' ", *The Invention of Ethnicity*, ed. by Werner Sollors, New York, Oxford U.P., 14-43
Calmet, Augustin	1832	*Calmet's Dictionary of the Bible*, Boston, Crocker and Brewster
Castle, Terry	1988	"Phantasmagoria: Spectral Technology and the Metaphorics of Modern Reverie", *Critical Inquiry*, 15, 1, 26-61
Carlyle, Thomas	1969	*Sartor Resartus*, New York, AMS Press
	1989	*The French Revolution*, 3 vols., London, The Folio Society
Chako, David; Kulchsar, Alexander	1984	"Israel Potter: Genesis of a Legend", *William and Mary Quarterly*, 4, 2, 364-389.
Clapp, William	1853	*Record of the Boston Stage*, Boston, James Munroe & Co.
Cohen, Hennig	1986	"Israel Potter: Common Man as Hero", *A Companion to Melville Studies*, ed. by John Bryant, New York, Greenwood Press, 279-313
	1991	*Israel Potter*, New York, Fordham U.P., edited, with notes and introduction
Colacurcio, Michael J.	1984	*The Province of Piety: Moral History in Hawthorne's Early Tales*, Cambridge, Harvard U.P.
Cowen, Walker	1988	*Melville's Marginalia*, 2 vols., New York, Garland
Crary Jonathan	1990	*Techniques of the Observer, On Vision and Modernity in the Nineteenth Century*, Cambridge, MIT Press
Crawford, Martin	1987	*The Anglo-American Crisis of the Mid-Nineteenth Century, "The Time" and America, 1850-1862*, Athens, University of Georgia Press

Crews, Frederick | 1966 | *The Sins of the Father: Hawthorne's Psychological Themes*, New York, Oxford U.P.

Crowley, Donald J. | 1970 | *Hawthorne: The Critical Heritage*, London, Routledge.

Cumming, Mark | 1988 | *A Disimprisoned Epic*, Philadelphia, University of Pennsylvania Press

Dauber, Kenneth | 1977 | *Rediscovering Hawthorne*, Princeton, Princeton U.P.

Davidson, Edward H. | 1949 | *Hawthorne's Last Phase*, New Haven, Yale U.P.

1964 | "The Unfinished Romances", *Hawthorne Centenary Essays*, Columbus, Ohio State U.P., 141-63

Dekker, George | 1987 | *The American Historical Romance*, Cambridge, Cambridge U.P.

De Quincey, Thomas | 1851 | *Confessions of an Opium-Eater and Suspiria de Profundis*, Boston, Ticknor

Dillingham, William B. | 1986 | *Melville's Later Novels*, Athens, University of Georgia Press

Dods, John B. | 1850 | *The Philosophy of Electrical Psychology*, New York, Fowlers and Wells

Dorson, Richard | 1953 | *American Rebels*, New York, Pantheon Books

Dryden, Edgar A. | 1968 | *Melville's Thematics of Form: The Great Art of Telling the Truth*, Baltimore, Johns Hopkins University Press

Edel, Leon | 1974 | *Henry James: Letters*, 1, Cambridge, Harvard U.P.

Eliot, T.S. | 1963 | *Collected Poems*, London, Faber and Faber

Ellenberger Henry F. | 1970 | *The Discovery of the Unconscious*, New York, Basic Books

Ellis, George E. | 1843 | *Sketches of Bunker Hill Battle and Monument*, Charlestown, Emmons

Emerson, Ralph Waldo | 1982 | *Emerson in His Journals*, ed. by Joel Porte, Cambridge, Harvard U.P.

1983 | *Essays and Lectures*, New York, The Library of America

Erlich Gloria | 1984 | *Family Themes and Hawthorne's Fiction*, New Brunswick, Rutgers U.P.

Everett, Edward | 1836 | *Orations and Speeches*, Boston, American Stationers

Field, David D. | 1829 | *A History of the County of Berkshire*, Pittsfield, S.W. Bush

Field, Henry M. | 1860 | *History of the Atlantic Telegraph*, New York, Scribners

Fink, Guido | 1990 | "Hawthorne e i fantasmi della libertà", *Leggende del Palazzo del Governatore*, Venezia, Marsilio, 9-37

Flibbert, Joseph   1974   *Melville and the Art of Burlesque*, Amsterdam, Rodopi

Foner, Philip S.   1976   *We, the Other People*, Chicago, University of Illinois Press

Forgie, George B.   1979   *Patricide in the House Divided*, New York, Norton

Foucault, Michel   1965   *Madness and Civilization*, New York, Random House

Frederick, John T.   1962   "Symbol and Theme in Israel Potter", *Modern Fiction Studies*, 8, 3, 1962, 265-275

Freud, Sigmund   1974   *Beyond the Pleasure Principle*, 18, London, Hogarth Press

Frothingham, Richard   1896   *History of the Siege of Boston and of the Battles of Lexington, Concord and Bunker Hill*, Boston, Little & Brown

Froude, James A.   1882   *Thomas Carlyle*, 1, London, Longmans

Fuller, Robert C.   1982   *Mesmerism and the American Cure*, Philadelphia, University of Pennsylvania Press

Fussell, Edwin   1965   *American Literature and the American West*, Princeton, Princeton U.P.

Gilmore, Michael T.   1977   *The Middle Way: Puritanism and Ideology in American Romantic Fiction*, New Brunswick, Rutgers U.P.

Graves, Robert   1955   *The Greek Myths*, 1, Harmondsworth, Penguin

Grimes, Stanley J.   1850   *Etherology & Phreno-Philosophy*, Boston, Munroe

Hall, David   1989   *Worlds of Wonders, Days of Judgements*, Cambridge, Harvard U.P.

Hartman, Geoffrey   1986   "Enthusiastic Criticism", *Thomas Carlyle*, ed. by Harold Bloom, New York, Chelsea House, 121-6

Hawthorne, Nathaniel   1883   "Chiefly About War Matters", 12, Boston, Houghton and Mifflin, 299-345

    1962   *The English Notebooks*, New York, Russell & Russell

    1970   *Our Old Home*, 5, Columbus, Ohio State U.P.

    1972   *The American Notebooks*, 8, Columbus, Ohio State U.P.

    1977   *The American Claimant Manuscripts*, 12, Columbus, Ohio State U.P.

    1977   *The Elixir of Life Manuscripts*, 13, Columbus, Ohio State U.P.

    1980   *The French and Italian Notebooks*, 14, Columbus, Ohio State U.P.

	1982	*Tales and Sketches*, New York, The Library of America
	1983	*Novels*, New York, The Library of America
Heimert, Alan	1963	"Moby Dick and American Political Symbolism", *American Quarterly*, 15, 499-534
Henderson, Harry B.	1974	*Versions of the Past, The Historical Imagination in American Fiction*, New York, Oxford U.P.
Higham, John	1981	*Strangers in the Land*, Westport, Greenwood Press
Hitchens, Christopher	1990	*Blood, Class, and Nostalgia*, New York, Farrar
Hobsbawm, Eric; Ranger, Terence (eds).	1983	*The Invention of Tradition*, Cambridge, Cambridge U.P
Holmes, Oliver W.	1975	*The Poetical Works*, Boston, Houghton Mifflin
James, Henry	1945	*The Sense of the Past*, New York, Scribners
	1967	*Hawthorne*, New York, Macmillan
	1984	*Essays on Literature: American Writers, English Writers*, New York, The Library of America
James, William	1981	*The Principles of Psychology*, Cambridge, Harvard U.P.
	1986	*Essays in Psychical Research*, Cambridge, Harvard U.P.
Kammen, Michael	1978	*A Season of Youth: the American Revolution and the Historical Imagination*, New York, Knopf.
	1991	*Mystic Chords of Memory: The Transformation of Tradition in American Culture*, New York, Knopf
Karcher, Carolyn L.	1980	*Shadow over the Promised Land: Slavery, Race and Violence in Melville's America*, Baton Rouge, Louisiana State U.P.
Kesserling, Marion L.	1949	*Hawthorne's Readings, 1828-1850*, New York, New York Public Library
Keyssar, Alexander	1969	*Melville's Israel Potter: Reflections on the American Dream*, Cambridge, Harvard U.P.
Koselleck, Reinhart	1985	*Future Past*, Cambridge, MIT Press
Lanati, Barbara	1987	*Frammenti di un sogno*, Milano, Feltrinelli
Lease, Benjamin	1976	"Hawthorne and the Archeology of the Cinema", *The Nathaniel Hawthorne Journal*, 1976, 132-171
Lombardo, Agostino	1961	*La ricerca del vero*, Roma, Edizioni di Storia e Letteratura
	1976	*Un rapporto col mondo, saggio sui racconti di N. Hawthorne*, Roma, Bulzoni
Lotman, Yury	1976	*Analysis of the Poetic Text*, Ann Arbor, Ardis

Lowenthal, David 1985 *The Past is a Foreign Country*, Cambridge, Cambridge U.P.

Lukács, Georg 1981 "The Metaphysics of Tragedy", *Tragedy, Vision and Form*, ed. by Robert W. Corrigan, New York, Harper & Row, 76-93

Lundblad, Jane 1965 *Nathaniel Hawthorne and European Literary Tradition*, New York, Russell & Russell

Madison, R.D. 1982 "Related Document", *Israel Potter*, Chicago, Northwestern U.P., 277-85

Mansfield, L.; Vincent, H.P. (eds) 1962 *Moby Dick*, New York, Hendricks House

Materassi, Mario 1983 "L'idolo nell'occhio: una analisi di Benito Cereno", *Melvilliana*, ed. by Paola Cabibbo, Roma, Bulzoni, 79-107

Matthiessen, F.O. 1941 *American Renaissance*, New York, Oxford U.P.

McWilliams, John P. 1984 *Hawthorne, Melville and the American Character*, Cambridge, Cambridge U.P.

Melchiori, Barbara; Melchiori, Giorgio 1974 *Il gusto di Henry James*, Torino, Einaudi

Mellow, James 1980 *Nathaniel Hawthorne in His Times*, Boston, Houghton Mifflin

Melville, Herman 1948 *Journal of a Visit to London and the Continent*, ed. by Eleanor Metcalf Melville, Cambridge, Harvard U.P.

1982 *Israel Potter*, Chicago, Northwestern U.P.

1983 *Redburn, White-Jacket, Moby-Dick*, New York, The Library of America

1984 *Pierre, Israel Potter, The Piazza Tales, The Confidence Man, Uncollected Prose, Billy Budd*, New York, The Library of America

Mercier, Sebastien 1800 *Nouveau Paris*, Brunswick, Les Principaux Librairies

Miller, Edwin H. 1991 *Salem is My Dwelling Place, A Life of Nathaniel Hawthorne*, Iowa City, University of Iowa Press

Miller, Hillis J. 1991 *Hawthorne and History: Defacing It*, Cambridge, Blackwell

Mizruchi, Susan L. 1988 *The Power of Historical Knowledge*, Princeton, Princeton U.P.

Montague, Émile 1860 "Un romancier pessimiste en Amérique", *Revue des deux mondes*, XXVIII, 668-703

Morley, Malcolm 1952 "Pepper and the Haunted Man", *The Dickensian*, 48, 185-90

Newberry, Frederick   1989   *Hawthorne's Divided Loyalties, England and America in His Works*, Rutherford, Farleigh Dickinson U.P.

Normand, Jean   1970   *Nathaniel Hawthorne, An Approach to an Analysis of Artistic Creation*, Cleveland, Case Western Reserve University Press

Pagnini, Marcello   1970   *Critica della funzionalità*, Torino, Einaudi

Pearce, Roy H.   1964   "Romance and the Study of History", *Hawthorne Centenary Essays*, Columbus, Ohio U.P., 221-44

Penn Warren, Robert; et al. (eds)   1973   *American Literature: The Makers and the Making*, New York, St Martin Press

Perosa, Sergio   1978   *Henry James and the Experimental Novel*, Charlottesville, University Press of Virginia

    1984   *American Theories of the Novel*, New York, New York U.P.

Pettus Hay, Marcus   1967   *Nation's Jubilee: One Hundred Years of the Fourth of July*, DA, University of Kentucky

Pfister, Joel   1991   *The Production of Personal Life*, Stanford, Stanford U.P.

Placido, Beniamino   1975   *Le due schiavitù*, Torino, Einaudi

Poe, Edgar A.   1984   *Marginalia, Essays and Reviews*, New York, The Library of America

Poulet, Georges   1968   *Mesure de l'instant*, Paris, Éditions du Rocher

Rampersad, Arnold   1969   *Melville's Israel Potter: A Pilgrimage and a Progress*, Bowling Green, Bowling Green University Popular Press

Ricoeur, Paul   1984   *Narrative Time*, Chicago, University of Chicago Press

Robertson, Etienne G.   1831   *Mémoires: récréatifs, scientifique, et anedoctyque d'un physicien-aéronaute*, 1, Paris, priv. print.

Robotti, Frances D.   1948   *Chronicles of Old Salem: A History in Miniature*, Salem, Newcomb and Gauss

Rogin, Paul M.   1983   *Subversive Genealogy: The Politics and Art of Herman Melville*, New York, Knopf

Rosenberg, Brian   1987   "*Israel Potter*: Melville's Anti-History", *Studies in American Fiction*, 15, 175-86

Ryan, Pat M.   1958   "Young Hawthorne at the Salem Theatre", *Essex Institute Historical Collections*, 14, 243-55

Samson, John   1989   *White Lies: Melville's Narratives of Facts*, Ithaca, Cornell U.P.

Santayana, George   1905   *The Life of Reason and Human Progress*, 1, London, Constable

Schneewind, J.B., ed. 1965 *Mill's Essays on Nature and Society*, New York, Collier

Scott, Walter 1895 *Old Mortality*, London , Constable

Sealts, Merton 1988 *Melville's Reading*, Columbia, University of South Carolina Press

Shaw, Peter 1981 *American Patriots and the Rituals of Revolution*, Cambridge, Harvard U.P.

Sherrill, Rowland A. 1979 *The Prophetic Melville*, Athens, University of Georgia Press

Sonneck, O.G.T. 1914 *The Star Spangled Banner*, Washington, Government Printing Office

Smith, Grover 1956 *T.S. Eliot's Poetry and Plays, A Study in Sources and Meanings*, Chicago, University of Chicago Press

Stoehr, Taylor 1978 *Hawthorne's Mad Scientists*, Hamden, Archon Books

Sumner, Charles 1845 *The True Grandeur of Nations*, Boston, Eastburn

Sundquist, Eric J. 1986 "Benito Cereno and New World Slavery", *Reconstructing American Literary History*, ed. by S. Bercovitch, Cambridge, Harvard U.P., 93-122

Swann, Charles 1991 *Nathaniel Hawthorne, Tradition and Revolution*, Cambridge, Cambridge U.P.

Thoreau, Henry D. 1970 *The Annotated Walden*, ed. by Philip Van Doren Stern, New York, Clarkson N. Potter Inc./ Publisher

1985 *A Week on the Concord and Merrimack Rivers*, New York, The Library of America

Townshend, Chauncy H. 1854 *Mesmerism Proved True*, London, Bosworth

Trilling, Lionel 1964 "Our Hawthorne", *Hawthorne Centenary Essays*, Columbus, Ohio U.P., 429-58

Trumbull, Henry 1982 *Life and Remarkable Adventures of Israel Potter, Israel Potter*, Chicago, Northwestern U.P., 286-394

Webster, Daniel 1851 *Works*, Boston, Little and Brown

1895 *Daniel Webster's First Bunker Hill Oration*, ed. by Fred Scott, New York, Longmans

Whipple, Edwin P. 1860 "Nathaniel Hawthorne", *Atlantic Monthly*, 5, 614-22

White, Hayden 1987 *The Content of Form*, Baltimore, The Johns Hopkins U.P.

Whitman, Walt 1982 *Poetry and Prose*, New York, The Library of America

Williams, William C. 1956 *In the American Grain*, New York, New Directions

Wright, Nathalia 1949 *Melville's Use of the Bible*, Durham, Duke U.P.

Zaller, Robert	1976	"Melville and the Myth of Revolution", *Studies in Romanticism*, 15, 3, 607-22
Zelinsky, Wilbur	1988	*Nation into State*, Chapel Hill, University of North Carolina Press